COLLEGE VOCABULARY SKILLS

W9-BUE-806

© 1979 by Houghton Mifflin Company

COLLEGE VOCABULARY SKILLS

James F. Shepherd

Queensborough Community College,
The City University of New York

PROPERTY OF
COMMUNICATION SKILLS CENTER
OHIO NORTHERN UNIVERSITY

Houghton Mifflin Company   Boston
Dallas   Geneva, Illinois   Hopewell, New Jersey
Palo Alto   London

This book is dedicated to Waldo and Lillian Hancock, Joseph
and Dorothy Hosey, Sumner and Josephine Ives, Leonard
and Lucile Martin, Clem and Koreyne Simpson, Robert and
Diane Steffer, and Loyd and Mary Elizabeth Waltz.

Cover illustration by Tonia Noell-Roberts

All dictionary entries reproduced in this text are from either the desk or the paperback
edition of the *American Heritage Dictionary of the English Language*. Entries from
desk edition © 1969, 1970, 1971, 1973, 1975, 1976, 1978, Houghton Mifflin Company.
Reprinted by permission from *The American Heritage Dictionary of the English Language*. Entry from Dell paperback edition © 1969, 1970, 1973, 1976, Houghton Mifflin
Company. Reprinted by permission from *The American Heritage Dictionary of the
English Language,* paperback edition.

Copyright © 1979 by Houghton Mifflin Company. All rights reserved. No part of this
work may be reproduced or transmitted in any form or by any means, electronic or
mechanical, including photocopying and recording, or by any information storage or
retrieval system, without permission in writing from the publisher.

Printed in the U.S.A.

Library of Congress Catalog Card Number: 78-69548

ISBN: 0-395-26851-6

CONTENTS

© 1979 by Houghton Mifflin Company

© 1979 by Houghton Mifflin Company

PREFACE

College Vocabulary Skills was written to teach what educated Americans should know about English words. It provides students with the information, strategies, and skills that are most likely to ensure them a lifetime of vocabulary growth.

This book is the result of many years of teaching experience and extensive language research that began while I was writing a dissertation on English morphology. Those were difficult but joyous days—difficult because of the exigencies of dissertation writing; joyous because it was then that I fell in love with English words. Though I had been an English major in college and had taught English for several years, it was in mid-life that I discovered how to focus my attention and so develop a deep and abiding interest in words. In writing this book I have attempted to open for others the doors that were opened for me long after I thought I had become an educated person; I have tried to make this book suitable for anybody who wants or needs to acquire a larger vocabulary.

In Part I, eleven chapters teach students how to use context, word structure, and reference sources to find the meanings of words so that they may increase their *reading and listening vocabulary;* in Part II, five chapters instruct them how to learn systematically the meanings, pronunciations, spellings, etymologies, and synonyms of words so that they may include new words in their *writing and speaking vocabulary.* The book is arranged in a logical sequence, but it is also logical to study the chapters in Part II before or at the same time as the chapters in Part I; it is logical to begin today to move words from the reading and listening vocabulary into the writing and speaking vocabulary. Also, the chapters

x

© 1979 by Houghton Mifflin Company

have been written so that when students need improvement in specific skills, they may study a chapter that involves those skills without first studying other chapters.

Each chapter begins with an explanation of basic concepts written so it can be easily understood by almost all college freshmen and concludes with enough problems or exercises to ensure that students will acquire desired understandings, strategies, and skills. This format makes *College Vocabulary Skills* suitable for use in reading, writing, and study-skills classrooms as well as in skills centers and laboratories. In addition, when self-motivated students are provided with the answers to the exercises, they can have a successful learning experience when they study this book independently.

The exercises in *College Vocabulary Skills* are not difficult to do; they are only as difficult as they must be to serve the instructional purposes for which they are intended. The correct level of difficulty was achieved through careful field testing, using as a model for exercise difficulty the exercises in Norman C. Stageberg's *An Introductory English Grammar*. It would please me if students who use *College Vocabulary Skills* have as pleasurable and significant a learning experience as I did when I studied Professor Stageberg's book in 1967.

Many readers will induce the linguists who have influenced me most, but they may not readily recognize that I learned a great deal from obscure works by John B. Carroll, Lee C. Deighton, Hans Marchand, and Edward L. Thorndike.

I thank the following reviewers for the comments they offered about this book when it was in manuscript form and for the suggestions they made for its improvement: Paul Dudenhefer of the State Technical Institute at Memphis, Edward J. Griffin of Nassau Community College, Ralph H. Huhn, Jr., of McNeese State University, Madeline S. Nixon of St. Petersburg Junior College, Delores Ridenour of Loraine County Community College, Barbara Dickson Sussman of Miami-Dade Community College, and Edward F. Wightman of Hudson Valley Community College.

Also, I thank my colleagues Professors Elaine Morton and Joseph Hosey for field testing *College Vocabulary Skills;* their wisdom has enriched me greatly.

Finally, I acknowledge my good fortune to have as friends the outstanding teachers to whom I have dedicated this book. In tribute to them all, I especially thank the two who have helped me most in understanding language and the teaching of language: Sumner and Josephine Ives, Professors Emeritus of New York University. I have benefited more than I can say from the unselfish counsel of these two seekers after truth.

J.F.S.

© 1979 by Houghton Mifflin Company

TO THE STUDENT

A famous singer used to end her nightclub act by saying, "That's all there is, there isn't any more." The same cannot be said of English words. The number of words in the English language is already so large that nobody could possibly learn all those words in a lifetime, and new words are added to our language every year.

In the preface to this book, I tell that in my mid-thirties, though I thought I was well educated in the English language, I had not yet developed a deep interest in words. I had lived half a lifetime, and though I had learned what to attend to so I could enjoy sports, theater, books, and many other joys of life, I had not learned what to attend to so I could get pleasure from words. Then I became involved in language research that led me to understand the ways I should focus my attention on words—the ways I should attend to words to find their fascination.

You may be younger than I was when I first fell in love with words. I wrote this book so that you would learn early in your college career how to attend to words and thus to enjoy them. If I knew anything else to tell you about how you can engage in a love affair with words, I would. But I can think of no ways to expand your vocabulary other than the ones I present to you in this book. If you study this book attentively, you will learn how you can increase the number of words you recognize and use. There will always be more words to learn. You will never be able to say, "That's all there is, there isn't any more." But when you have done the exercises in this book, you will at least know the strategies you may use to continue adding new words fairly easily to your vocabulary.

We can lose much of what we have in life. Our money, our health, our loved ones can be with us one day and gone the next. But the great treasure of the English language cannot be taken from us. It would please me greatly to know that what you will have learned when you have finished studying *College Vocabulary Skills* has helped you to develop a greater interest in English words. It would please me even more if I should learn that by using what you study here, you have set an example for somebody else and have thus helped another find the endless pleasure that words can give.

J.F.S.

© 1979 by Houghton Mifflin Company

Chapter 1

Introduction: Two Types of Vocabularies

You may think of yourself as having one vocabulary, but in fact you have several vocabularies! You probably have a slang vocabulary that you use with your friends, an informal vocabulary that you use with your family, and a more formal vocabulary that you use when you transact important business, visit a doctor, or write papers for college courses. In addition, you have the two types of vocabularies that are of special interest in this book: (1) the words you *know* when you read or listen and (2) the words you *use* when you write or speak. These are sometimes called the *receptive vocabulary* (words you "receive" when you read and listen) and *expressive vocabulary* (words you use to "express" yourself when you write and speak).

These two vocabularies are quite different in size. There are many words that you know when you read and listen but never use when you write or speak; your receptive vocabulary is several times larger than your expressive vocabulary. But in one respect these two vocabularies of yours are identical: *No matter how small or large your receptive and expressive vocabularies are, they can both become larger—much larger!* There are more than 500,000 words in the English language, and it is estimated that average well-educated Americans make practical use of only about 30,000 of these words.

Thus, when you do your college study, you must expect that any one of some 470,000 words that you have never seen or heard before may suddenly appear. You must have at your command a variety of techniques to use to identify quickly and accurately the meanings of most of these words so that you will understand what is written in your books or spoken in your lectures. Also, in college you will be called on to express your ideas in writing and in class discussions. Unless you have a large writing and speaking vocabulary, these demands are likely to be endlessly frustrating to you.

These, then, are two questions that every person who wants to become better educated must ask:

1. How can I quickly find the meanings of the new words that I encounter when I read and listen?
2. How can I acquire the words I need to express my thoughts when I write and speak?

This book was written to help you find the answers to these questions.

THE BASIC PLAN OF THIS BOOK

The overall plan of this book was developed from the following reasoning:

1. If you do not know a word when you read it or hear it, you cannot use the word when you write or speak.
2. If you have a *large* reading and listening vocabulary, you have the potential for having a large writing and speaking vocabulary; if you have a *small* reading and listening vocabulary, there is no way you can have a large writing and speaking vocabulary.
3. Since the number of words you use when you write and speak is directly related to the number of words you know when you read and listen, it is especially important for you to increase the size of your reading and listening vocabulary.

The ten chapters in Part I of this book will help you understand how the use of context, word structure, and reference sources can help you increase your reading and listening vocabulary, and the five chapters in Part II will help you discover how to learn meanings, pronunciations, spellings, and synonyms for words you wish to add to your writing and speaking vocabulary.

© 1979 by Houghton Mifflin Company

HOW TO USE THIS BOOK

The chapters in this book are arranged in a logical order for study. However, while it is appropriate to study them in the order in which they are presented, it is also logical to study the chapters in Part II (Increasing Your Writing and Speaking Vocabulary) either before or at the same time as you study Part I (Increasing Your Reading and Listening Vocabulary). Also, most of the chapters have been written so they may be studied independently of other chapters.

Explanations. Each chapter contains explanations that were written for *you* to read. The explanations help you understand the purposes of the exercises and provide you with information you may not find elsewhere. If you read the explanations carefully, you should learn skills you can use during your college years and throughout your lifetime to help you find and learn the meanings of words.

Exercises. Each chapter (except this one) contains an exercise or set of exercises that help you learn about words by working with words. *The exercises are not supposed to be difficult; if you do them carefully, you should almost always be able to solve most of the problems correctly.* The purpose of the exercises is to focus your attention on important things that you should understand about words, not to confuse or bewilder you. *If you do the exercises carefully, you should learn most of the things well-educated people should know about English words.*

Answer Key. At the end of the book you will find an answer key that gives the answers to *some* of the problems: it is not a complete answer key. The answers given there are intended to help you when you have difficulty understanding exactly how you are to solve the problems for an exercise. If you write answers that are different from the ones in the answer key, you will know you are doing something incorrectly. You should then reread the explanation in the text.

© 1979 by Houghton Mifflin Company

PART I INCREASING YOUR READING AND LISTENING VOCABULARY

Many people believe that if they read or hear a word they do not know, they must look for its meaning in a dictionary. However, there are actually four basic ways in which people may increase their reading and listening vocabulary: (1) by studying context, (2) by studying word structure, (3) by using reference sources—not necessarily a dictionary, and (4) by asking somebody for the meanings of words.

Finding Word Meanings in Context. A context is a written or spoken statement that may reveal the meaning of a word. The meaning of *thespians* is revealed in the context of the following sentence:

> Many English **thespians** are well known in this country because they have acted on the Broadway stage or in motion pictures.

What are thespians?

Even if you had never seen the word before, it should have been easy for you to determine that thespians are actors. The meaning of *thespians* is revealed in the context of the sentence. *Chapters 2, 3, and 4* will help you increase your ability to find word meanings from context.

Finding Word Meanings in Word Structure. A second way to find word meanings without referring to a dictionary is to analyze the structure of words. Can you use word structure to find the meaning of this word?

p s e u d o s c i e n c e

What is the meaning of *pseudoscience?*

In order to find the meaning of this word, you need to know that the prefix *pseudo-* means "false." A pseudoscience is a false science, such as astrology. If you understand word structure, you can use it to unlock the meanings of thousands of words without consulting a dictionary. Because of its importance, much attention is given to word structure in *Chapters 5, 6, 7, 8, and 9.* Those chapters teach about prefixes, base words, suffixes, and combining forms.

Finding Word Meanings in Reference Sources. When it is not possible to determine the meaning of a word by studying context or word structure, it is usually necessary to consult a dictionary or other reference source. *Chapter 10* provides information and practice to help you overcome any difficulties you may have in finding the meanings of words in dictionaries. However, there will be times when a dictionary will not give you all the information you want about a word, and you will find that many words are not defined even in good desk dictionaries. *Chapter 11* explains how to use encyclopedias, specialized dictionaries, and other books to find the kinds of information about a word that desk dictionaries do not give.

Finding Word Meanings by Asking Somebody. There is no chapter on the fourth way to find out what a word means. But we do sometimes forget that we can find the meanings of words simply by asking somebody what they mean. This was a primary source of information about word meanings for us when we were young, but we tend to stop asking for word meanings as we grow older.

Your college teachers are experts on the meanings of words that they use in their lectures or that appear in books you read in their courses. Most teachers are willing, even eager, to explain the meanings of words that are important to their subject matter. Keep in mind that your professors are a valuable resource to you if you wish to increase your reading and listening vocabulary; ask them for the meanings of words you need to know in order to understand their course work.

© 1979 by Houghton Mifflin Company

SECTION 1

FINDING WORD MEANINGS IN CONTEXT

A *context* is a written or spoken statement that may reveal the meaning of a word. For example:

> Your **receptive vocabulary** is the words you know when you read or listen, and your **expressive vocabulary** is the words you use when you write or speak.

The meanings of *receptive vocabulary* and *expressive vocabulary* are revealed in the context of this sentence.

In college you will need to know the meanings of hundreds of words you have never seen or heard before; if you are skillful in using context to find word meanings, you will not need to consult a dictionary every time you encounter an unknown word.

Chapter 2 explains four different ways the meanings of words are revealed in sentences; *Chapter 3* demonstrates how the meanings of words are revealed in the longer passages of textbooks; and *Chapter 4* illustrates how the meanings of words are sometimes revealed by pictures. Each chapter contains practice to help you become more skillful in using context to find the meanings of words.

Chapter 2   Finding Word Meanings in Sentences

Before you read any part of this chapter, test yourself to see if you know the meanings of the following words by printing *a*, *b*, *c*, or *d* in the first column of blank lines:

___ ___ 1. supersede   a. retrieve   b. review
                         c. replace   d. recede

___ ___ 2. surrogate   a. openness   b. substitute
                         c. legal   d. courtly

___ ___ 3. prerogative   a. order   b. right
                         c. dispatch   d. honesty

___ ___ 4. panacea   a. truth   b. glue
                         c. cure   d. cake

___ ___ 5. thwart   a. aid   b. cut
                         c. twitch   d. block

___ ___ 6. contiguous   a. bordering   b. extended
                         c. opposite   d. broken

___ ___ 7. tryst   a. meeting   b. trick
                         c. drama   d. growth

___ ___ 8. peccadillo   a. sword   b. cigar
                         c. punch   d. fault

A *context* is a written or spoken statement that may help one determine the meanings of unknown words. The meanings of the eight words listed above are revealed in the contexts of the following sentences. Read the sentences to find the meanings. If you

© 1979 by Houghton Mifflin Company

change your mind about the meaning of any of the words, indicate your changed answers in the second column of blanks above.

1. The new tax law **supersedes,** or replaces, the law that was in effect last year.

2. Psychologists have learned that parentless infant monkeys will use any object, even a glove, as a **surrogate** mother—a substitute parent.

3. We all have the right to have our own opinions and the **prerogative** to express our points of view.

4. It would be foolhardy to leave town as a **panacea** for your difficulties, because running away will not remedy your problems.

5. At one time there was no way to prevent people from hijacking airplanes, but now precautionary measures have been taken to **thwart** such misadventures.

6. California is **contiguous** to Nevada; however, it is hundreds of miles from Colorado.

7. Amelia's parents disapproved of her boyfriend, so she planned **trysts** with him in restaurants or in the homes of friends.

8. Nesbit's poor table manners are a **peccadillo** we shall overlook, as his fine conversation more than makes up for the annoyance of listening to him slurp his soup.

Even though the meanings of the eight words are given in the sentences, some people have difficulty finding them. The correct answers to the questions are: 1, c; 2, b; 3, b; 4, c; 5, d; 6, a; 7, a; 8, d. Whether or not you found all the correct answers, you will make better use of context after you study this chapter.

FOUR CLUES TO MEANING THAT ARE FOUND IN CONTEXT

When you begin reading books and articles in a new college subject, you are likely to come across many words you do not know. If you are forced to consult a dictionary for the meanings of many unfamiliar words, you will be greatly slowed down and you probably will not find much enjoyment in reading. Knowing the four ways in which meanings of words can be revealed in context will increase your ability to determine the meanings of unknown words without referring to a dictionary. These four ways are

1. restatement with punctuation,
2. restatement without punctuation,
3. restatement in contrast, and
4. general sense.

Each of these is discussed in the pages that follow.

Restatement With Punctuation. When writers use words that they believe may not be known to all readers, they often set off the meanings of such words with commas, dashes, parentheses, or other punctuation marks. For example, a writer who needs to use the word *prosthesis* may anticipate that some readers will not know its meaning and so may restate the meaning, enclosing it in punctuation:

> John was given a **prosthesis** (an artificial arm) to replace the limb he lost in the accident.

In this case the writer used parentheses to restate the meaning, but in sentences toward the beginning of this chapter the meaning of *supersede* was restated within commas and the meaning of *surrogate* was set off by a dash:

> The new tax law **supersedes,** or replaces, the law that was in effect last year.

> Psychologists have learned that parentless infant monkeys will use any object, even a glove, as a **surrogate** mother—a substitute parent.

The technique of setting off word meanings within punctuation is a very common one that you will notice in newspapers, magazines, textbooks, and many other types of reading materials.

Restatement Without Punctuation. When the meaning of a word is restated and set off by punctuation, it is quite clear that the writer intended to give the meaning. When a meaning is given without being set off within punctuation, it is not clear whether the

© 1979 by Houghton Mifflin Company

writer intended to give the meaning, but it is given all the same. For example:

> The McDonnell Company supplies victims of amputation with artificial arms and other **prostheses.**

In the sentences at the beginning of this chapter, the words *prerogative* and *panacea* were restated, but not set off by punctuation:

> We all have the right to have our own opinions and the **prerogative** to express our points of view.

> It would be foolhardy to leave town as a **panacea** for your difficulties, because running away will not remedy your problems.

The exact meanings of words are probably revealed in context more frequently by this method than by any of the other three ways described in this chapter.

Restatement in Contrast. The third way in which word meanings may be revealed in context is by a contrast. For example:

> John's left arm is his own, but the other is a **prosthesis.**

We can tell from this sentence that John's right arm is not his own. Since we know it cannot be somebody else's arm, we conclude it must be an artificial arm, and thus we find the meaning of *prosthesis.*

At the beginning of this chapter, the meanings of *thwart* and *contiguous* were presented in sentences that contained contrasts to their meanings:

> At one time there was no way to prevent people from hijacking airplanes, but now precautionary measures have been taken to **thwart** such misadventures.

The meaning of *thwart* may be found in the contrast "at one time there was no way to prevent . . . but now." Now there is a way to *prevent, stop, hinder,* or *block* people from hijacking airplanes.

> California is **contiguous** to Nevada; however, it is hundreds of miles from Colorado.

If being hundreds of miles away is different from being contiguous, *contiguous* must mean "near," "next to," or "bordering."

General Sense. Sometimes the meanings of unknown words can be determined by the general sense of a passage, even though they are not restated in any way:

> John has learned to type, dial a telephone, and even eat with the hooks at the end of his **prosthesis**.

Since most people type, dial telephones, and eat without using hooks, we may assume John's *prosthesis* is an artificial hand or arm.

It is usually much more difficult to determine the exact meanings of words from the general sense of passages than it is to find meanings from the other types of context clues. At the beginning of this chapter, the meanings of the words *tryst* and *peccadillo* may have been determined from the general sense of sentences:

> Amelia's parents disapproved of her boyfriend, so she planned **trysts** with him in restaurants or in the homes of friends.

The meaning of *trysts* may be easily determined from this sentence because we know that people have *meetings* in restaurants and other places when they cannot meet at home. But the "general sense" context for *peccadillo* is more typical:

> Nesbit's poor table manners are a **peccadillo** we shall overlook, as his fine conversation more than makes up for the annoyance of listening to him slurp his soup.

If you did not know the exact meaning of *peccadillo,* this context would not have been very helpful to you in determining that it means "a small sin or fault." From this context you might have decided that *peccadilloes* are annoying table manners. This reveals one of the three major limitations of using context to find the meanings of words.

© 1979 by Houghton Mifflin Company

**LIMITATIONS OF CONTEXT
AS A CLUE TO MEANING**

There are three limitations in using context to determine the meanings of words. The first one has been illustrated using *peccadillo:*

> *The context may not reveal an exact meaning of a word, only enough of a meaning so you may continue reading without consulting a dictionary.*

From the clues "poor table manners" and "slurping his soup" you know that something is slightly wrong with Nesbit, but you are unlikely to give *peccadillo* its exact meaning—"a small sin or fault." You would have missed the subtlety intended by the writer, but you would have been correct enough in your interpretation of *peccadillo* to continue reading without becoming frustrated, without referring to a dictionary, and without losing much of the meaning intended by the writer.

The second important limitation of context has been illustrated by using the word *prosthesis* in this chapter:

> *Context seldom reveals the complete meaning of a word.*

In this chapter *prosthesis* always referred to an arm, so you might have concluded that a prosthesis is always an artificial arm. However, in a dictionary you would find that prostheses include artificial arms, legs, teeth, eyes, and other body parts.

The third limitation of context is found in the fact that many words have more than one meaning:

> *When words have more than one meaning, context reveals only one of the meanings.*

The word *convention,* for example, has several meanings, two of which are "a formal assembly or meeting of members" and "a practice or procedure widely observed by a group, especially to facilitate social intercourse." A context may reveal one, but not both, of these meanings. The first meaning cannot be determined from this sentence:

> Gentlemen always used to open car doors for women, but this is a **convention** that is disappearing from our society.

From this sentence we can understand that *convention* refers to "a practice observed by a group," but we cannot find its other meanings.

PRACTICE PROBLEMS

Because of the limitations in the ability of context to reveal the meanings of words, you should not expect that you will always find the exact meanings of the words printed in dark type in the practice problems. You should, though, usually be able to find a reasonable synonym to replace most of the words printed in dark type in the problems.

The exercises begin with a list of the words whose meanings will be revealed in contexts. Follow these directions to solve the problems:

1. Study the list of words at the beginning of an exercise and write the meanings of any words that you already know.
2. Read the contexts for the words and write a word or phrase that (a) gives the meaning of the word and (b) accurately replaces the word printed in dark type in the context.
3. *Do not use a dictionary to solve the problems;* this defeats the purpose of the exercises.

Following are three sample problems that have been solved to illustrate how they are to be done.

1. lexicon   *dictionary*

2. lethal   *deadly*

3. verbatim   *word for word*

1. We used an authoritative **lexicon** (dictionary) to settle disputes over preferred spellings and pronunciations of words.
2. By now most people know they can be killed by the **lethal** combination of tranquilizers and alcohol.
3. The judge asked if I was quoting her **verbatim** or if I was simply giving a general impression of what she said.

Please notice that the words printed in dark type in the sentences

© 1979 by Houghton Mifflin Company

have been defined in such a way that they may be removed from the sentences and replaced with their definitions:

1. We used an authoritative **dictionary** to settle disputes over preferred spellings and pronunciations of words.

2. By now most people know they can be killed by the **deadly** combination of tranquilizers and alcohol.

3. The judge asked if I was quoting her **word for word** or if I was simply giving a general impression of what she said.

PROPERTY OF
COMMUNICATION SKILLS CENTER
OHIO NORTHERN UNIVERSITY.

© 1979 by Houghton Mifflin Company

Exercise 1   *Restatement With Punctuation*

The directions for solving these problems are given under "Practice Problems."

1. taxonomy

2. objective

3. syntax

4. semantics

5. covert

6. overt

7. explicit

8. implicit

9. ensemble

10. hyperbole

11. alliteration

12. eidetic imagery

1. Biologists use an elaborate **taxonomy** (classification system) to categorize animals and plants.

2. Scientists attempt to be **objective**—report what is factual and real.

3. **Syntax** (grammar) refers to the rules used to put words together to create phrases and sentences.

4. One branch of linguistic inquiry is **semantics**—the science of meaning in language.

5. The psychological significance of a tic, such as eye blinking, is **covert**, or concealed, to the person who has the tic.

6. On the other hand, the interpretations to be placed on symptoms of personality disorders are **overt** (not hidden) to psychiatrists.

7. When people receive credit cards, it is **explicit**, or clearly stated, in the contracts they sign that they will pay for any merchandise or services they receive from using the cards.

(continued)

.

8. However, when creditors use credit cards to make specific purchases, it is **implicit**—understood though not stated—that in so doing they will comply with their obligations to pay for purchases.

9. In opera, soloists often join together to sing in an **ensemble**—a small group such as a trio or quartet.

10. To say "I could eat a horse" is to use **hyperbole,** or overstatement.

11. **Alliteration** (the repetition of initial word sounds) is heard in the title of Shakespeare's play *Love's Labour's Lost.*

12. **Eidetic imagery,** or photographic memory, is observed less frequently in normal children than in those who are mentally retarded.

© 1979 by Houghton Mifflin Company

Exercise 2

Restatement Without Punctuation

The directions for solving these problems are given just before the first exercise for this chapter.

1. edifice

2. surreptitiously

3. impeccable

4. prestige

5. progeny

6. rapport

7. geriatrics

8. suave

9. predatory

10. enmity

11. dote

12. celibate

_____

_____

_____

_____

_____

_____

_____

_____

_____

_____

_____

_____

1. The Sears Building in Chicago is now the world's tallest **edifice**.

2. He **surreptitiously** packed his clothing and secretly slipped away; his absence was not noticed for nearly two days.

3. She was admired for her **impeccable** manners as well as her faultless taste in clothing.

4. It is one thing to have influence in high places, but quite another to have **prestige** in places of power as well as with common people.

5. The offspring of one insect can number in the thousands, but most insects' **progeny** do not survive for long.

6. It is important for a speaker to establish good **rapport** with the audience, because the speaker and the audience will enjoy the experience more if a warm relationship has been developed.

7. The general practitioner advised them that their elderly mother should be taken to a doctor who specializes in **geriatrics**.

(*continued*)

8. He was very polished in dress, speech, and deportment; in fact, he was **suave** in all respects.

9. There is nothing more fearsome than a **predatory** mob preying on a place, destroying it, and taking whatever it can.

10. I can understand how he might have angered her, but I will never believe he was responsible for the **enmity** she shows in her hostile attitude toward him.

11. Everybody should love their children, but it is worrisome to see her **dote** on her son as she does.

12. In the Roman Catholic Church, priests take vows that they will not marry and nuns also take vows to be **celibate**.

© 1979 by Houghton Mifflin Company

Exercise 3

Restatement in Contrast

The directions for solving these problems are given just before the first exercise for this chapter.

1. enervated   _____

2. acquitted   _____

3. interred   _____

4. lucrative   _____

5. extemporaneously   _____

6. contrite   _____

7. exonerated   _____

8. herbivorous   _____

9. verbose   _____

10. digress   _____

11. concur   _____

12. conjecture   _____

1. Phil started the long-distance race full of strength, but after about eight miles he was **enervated** by the hot sun and had to drop out.

2. Both of them stood trial, but one was found guilty and sent to prison while the other was **acquitted.**

3. It was the woman's grim responsibility to decide if her husband's body should be cremated or **interred.**

4. Alex was making so little money selling encyclopedias from door to door that he decided to search for more **lucrative** employment.

5. It is easier to present a speech for which one is completely prepared than to give a speech **extemporaneously.**

6. The brothers' reactions to having stolen the car were quite different—one was **contrite** while the other was not sorry in the least.

(*continued*)

7. Most thought she was guilty, but the trial **exonerated** her of the charge that she had tried to steal money from her company.

8. Carnivorous animals eat meat, but **herbivorous** animals do not.

9. Some people are **verbose,** while others have the ability to express their thoughts in few words.

10. When giving a brief speech, it is better to develop one thought completely than to **digress** on a variety of thoughts.

11. Jan and I **concur** that we will have children, but we disagree as to when we should start our family.

12. We might **conjecture** that the systematic study of words will increase students' vocabularies, but we cannot be absolutely certain this will happen in every case.

© 1979 by Houghton Mifflin Company

Exercise 4

General Sense

The directions for solving these problems are given just before the first exercise for this chapter.

1. extricate

2. incensed

3. traverse

4. abscond

5. coveted

6. pilfered

7. deter

8. alleviate

9. stentorian

10. inculcate

11. allusion

12. treatise

1. Ben's automobile caught fire upon impact, but fortunately he was able to **extricate** himself from it before it exploded.

2. Maybe I'm foolish, but I was so **incensed** that Fred didn't invite me to his party that I haven't spoken to him in a month.

3. We drove out of our way to **traverse** the river by ferry rather than by bridge.

4. The treasurer was put under close observation, as it was suspected she had plans to **abscond** with the company's funds.

5. She so **coveted** youth and beauty that she went to Switzerland and had her face lifted.

6. One overhead expense of all large offices is the cost of pencils, paper, and pens that are **pilfered** by employees for their personal use.

7. Even though our football players had lost six games in a row, we admired them because their losses did not **deter** them from playing their very best.

(continued)

8. An aspirin, fresh air, or something to eat will often **alleviate** a minor headache.

9. Even without the aid of a microphone, his **stentorian** voice filled the huge auditorium.

10. Some parents try to **inculcate** an appreciation for the arts in their children by taking them to theaters, concert halls, and museums.

11. She calls me "the bear"; it's an **allusion** to the fact that I like to hug.

12. Darwin proposed the theory of evolution in a **treatise** that has become one of the most famous works of all time.

© 1979 by Houghton Mifflin Company

Chapter 3   Finding Word Meanings in Textbooks

One of the primary purposes of many magazine articles and books is to define words that are new or important in a given field of investigation. For example, the writer of a magazine article on vision problems might need to explain astigmatism, presbyopia, and other eye ailments. Similarly, the authors of college textbooks cannot discuss business, psychology, science, art, or any other subject without revealing the meanings of words that are important within that subject. Therefore, the meanings of words used in business are given in the context of business textbooks, the definitions of terms used in psychology are given in the context of psychology textbooks, and so on. This chapter makes clear how word meanings are explained in textbooks so that you can find their meanings without referring to a dictionary or other reference source.

DEFINITIONS IN CONTEXT

When textbooks explain the meanings of words in context, they usually do so in a straightforward manner. Usually, words defined in textbooks are printed in special type. Notice in the following paragraph from a business textbook that the terms *middleman,* *merchant middlemen,* and *facilitating middlemen* are printed in special type and that their meanings are explained:

> Anyone in a channel of distribution who helps to move goods from producer to consumer is said to be a *middleman.* There are two types of middlemen: the merchant middleman and the facilitating middleman. *Merchant*

middlemen take title to the goods they handle, and they make a profit only if the goods are profitably sold. *Facilitating middlemen* do not take title or own the goods. Because facilitating middlemen do not assume risks, they are usually compensated by a fixed amount, such as a commission or a set percentage of the value of the goods they help to move.*

The meanings of words given in textbooks are often similar to those given in dictionaries. Compare this dictionary definition of *middleman* to the definition given in the business textbook passage:

mid·dle·man (mĭd′l-măn′) *n., pl.* **-men** (-mĕn′). **1.** A trader who buys from producers and sells to retailers or consumers. **2.** An intermediary or go-between.

However, textbooks often give the meanings of terms that are not defined in desk dictionaries. For example, you will not find *merchant middlemen* and *facilitating middlemen* explained in a desk dictionary. Usually your textbooks are your best sources of information about the meanings of words that are important in the courses you take in college.

PRACTICE PROBLEMS

The problems for this chapter request you to find the meanings of words explained in textbook passages. The first problem is based on a passage entitled "Pricing and Pricing Strategies" from a business textbook. It should help you understand how textbooks give information about words in context. The second problem gives you an opportunity to find the meanings of words explained in a textbook you are studying in college.

*From MODERN BUSINESS, 2nd edition, by S. B. Rosenblatt, R. L. Bonnington, and B. E. Needles, Jr. Copyright © 1977 by Houghton Mifflin Company. Used by permission.

© 1979 by Houghton Mifflin Company

Exercise 1

Context and Textbooks

Read "Pricing and Pricing Strategies" on pages 29–33 to find the meanings of the following ten words. Write their meanings in the spaces provided.

WRITE MEANINGS HERE:

1. skim-the-cream pricing

2. penetration pricing

3. arbitrary pricing

4. cost-plus pricing

(continued)

5. markups

_____

_____

_____

_____

6. follow-the-leader
   pricing

_____

_____

_____

_____

7. odd-figure pricing

_____

_____

_____

_____

8. multiple pricing

_____

_____

_____

_____

9. customary pricing

_____

_____

_____

_____

10. price line

_____

_____

_____

_____

© 1979 by Houghton Mifflin Company

Passage to Be Used with Exercise 1

Pricing and Pricing Strategies

△ The fourth element of the marketing mix is *pricing*. Business people do not talk much about pricing and price objectives, for fear of government action and disclosure to competition. Pricing objectives may be easier to attain in industries where there are few firms or among the larger firms under monopolistic competition than among smaller businesses. Small firms may have a hard time reaching their goals because of the nature of competition in their industry.

In certain marketing situations, the marketing manager may not have to make pricing decisions. Under perfect competition, prices will be set by the interaction of the supply and the demand; the market itself will set the price. Under oligopoly, the manager may follow the lead of the largest firm and exercise little or no control over pricing. In pure monopoly, prices are likely to be regulated by government. (These market structures are discussed in detail in Chapter 2.) Let us look at situations where the marketing manager has a real decision to make and where pricing plays a larger part in the distribution process.

Skim-the-Cream Pricing

When a product is sold at the highest possible price it is said to be sold at *skim-the-cream pricing*. The price is maintained until sales begin to fall off; then it is reduced until "the cream" has been skimmed off another pricing level (see Figure 12-3).

Skimming works only when a product or service is distinctive or when a firm has some protection from competition, such as a strong

Figure 12-3 Price-skimming Strategy

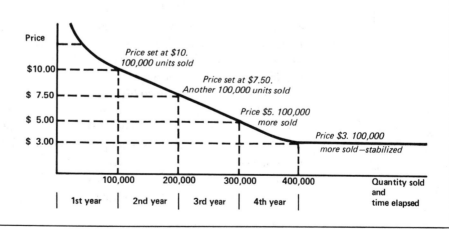

This passage is from MODERN BUSINESS, 2nd edition, by S. B. Rosenblatt, R. L. Bonnington, and B. E. Needles, Jr. Copyright © 1977 by Houghton Mifflin Company. Used by permission.

patent or a technological lead. A new motion picture, for example, may be shown only at the downtown theaters that charge a high admission. After the segment of the population that wants to see the film while it is new and talked about has been skimmed, the film may be moved to suburban theaters. When this market is exhausted, the movie may be shown at drive-in theaters at a still lower admission price. Finally, after several years, it is put on television at a still lower rental basis. Many products have been introduced this way: ball-point pens, Polaroid cameras, and color television sets, among others. Skim-the-cream pricing is a profit-maximizing strategy concerned more with the long-range than with the short-range sales potential.

Penetration Pricing

△ If a product is priced low enough or if the profit is kept at a barely satisfactory level, other producers will not be eager to enter, or penetrate, the market. Or so says the theory behind *penetration pricing*. Skim pricers may eventually reduce prices to this barely profitable level; penetration pricers start there. In Figure 12-3, the penetration price is $3. Products that can easily be produced and copied are subject to this price strategy. The McDonald's hamburger chain used penetration pricing when they entered the market. They sold hamburgers for fifteen cents, kept the profit margin low, and built a volume of sales that made it hard for competitors to follow the same pattern.

Arbitrary Pricing

Often prices result from arbitrary decisions. One decision is to charge "all the market can bear." The price maker sets a price at the upper limit of the demand in the expectation that a segment of the market will consider the product to be worth the price. Certain luxury goods such as jewelry, furs, and art may depend on such pricing to maintain their status. Because the market is exclusive, there is little chance for competition. What competition there is must be in terms of price or else the whole value of the item would be destroyed.

△ Another technique of *arbitrary pricing* of this sort is setting prices on the basis of a subjective assessment of how consumers will equate price and value. Most people have little knowledge of how much a seller pays for a product. Consumers judge fashionable clothing, for example, by how good they look in a particular outfit. A retail buyer who purchases an assortment of women's skirts may pay the same price for each. But, upon receiving and examining the skirts, the buyer may decide

© 1979 by Houghton Mifflin Company

(continued)

that some are more attractive than others and will command higher prices for these better-looking skirts. The buyer seeks to maximize profits by applying a value judgment to pricing.

Cost-Plus Pricing

Most retailers and wholesalers have little opportunity to alter pricing methods. National brands and even some entire industries customarily use given pricing formulas. For example, the producers of a certain brand of men's shirt advertise their product nationally at a suggested list, or selling, price of $10. It has been customary to sell this shirt to the retail store for 40 percent off list, so the retail store pays $6. Depending on the store's philosophy, the nature of the market, and the selling policies of the manufacturer, retailers may sell the shirt for any price over $6 and still make something above their cost. When they do this they △ are selling at *cost-plus pricing*.

If a wholesaler is part of the distribution channel—as is the case with most automobile parts, for example—the cost of the wholesale function is included in the original pricing. Suppose a spark plug has a suggested list price of $1.20, the retailer's trade discount is $33\frac{1}{3}$ percent of the list price, and the wholesaler's discount is 20 percent of the retail price. The wholesaler would pay the manufacturer $.64 for the spark plug and sell it to the retailer for $.80. The retailer would mark up its price, making it available to the consumer for $1.20. The discount or margin to the wholesaler and retailer should cover their costs and give them an acceptable profit.

△ *Markups* of the sort reflected in the price of the $1.20 spark plug and the $10 shirt are traditional in many industries, but discount stores, supermarkets, and other high-volume retailers may not sell goods at the manufacturer's suggested prices. A business concerned with rapid stock turnover may sell at lower prices in order to reach this objective and maximize profits. For example, a full-line hardware store must carry many items that are purchased infrequently and in small quantities. Suppose a hardware store keeps a $50,000 inventory. It has annual sales of $100,000, or a two-time annual turnover. In the same city, a discount store has a hardware department that has an average inventory of $20,000 and also does an annual volume of $100,000. The discount store has a five-time annual turnover. It does not stock all the items the hardware dealer does, but only those that sell rapidly and repeatedly. The discount store can charge lower prices because it operates at lower

(continued)

cost. It does not have as much capital tied up in inventory at one time as does the full-time hardware store.

Follow-the-Leader Pricing

Follow-the-leader is a pricing policy employed in many industries and many businesses. One company in an industry leads off, and all the others tend to follow. General Motors has been the price leader in the automotive oligopoly. It is generally the first to introduce new models, and the other manufacturers soon follow with competitive models priced at about the same level. Some years ago, Ford was first with new models and prices, and General Motors followed behind. As it happened, one Ford model cost about $100 more than the comparable GM car, and Ford soon reduced its price "to preserve competition." *Follow-the-leader pricing* is common where there are few producers and one giant among them.

Odd-Figure Pricing

Many people seem to think $19.95 is closer to $19 than it is to $20. Although they may hesitate to spend twenty dollars, they might spend nineteen dollars plus some odd change. As a result, we rarely see retail prices in round figures. Discount stores use a wide range of odd-figure prices to suggest greater bargains.

A form of this *odd-figure pricing* is *multiple pricing*, the offering of two or three or more of the same item at one price. This may be one way for a producer or merchant to sell more of the same goods. Three cans for $.89 somehow has the feel of a real bargain over one can at $.30 and indeed may offer a slight saving. People often find it hard to figure out cost per unit when seven packages cost $1.99.

Customary Prices

Over time, certain goods become associated with certain prices; these become the expected or *customary prices.* For years, soft drinks, candy bars, and chewing gum cost a nickel. Inflation and rising costs have forced the price of these items up, until today none of them sells for a nickel. Alternatives to raising these prices were sought for fear consumers would buy less at a higher price. Price setters carefully experimented before making any important changes. To test the market, soft drinks were first increased from five cents to seven cents. The increased price brought in greater total revenue, and the price was raised to ten cents and still met no resistance. Today, there are no customary prices.

The Price Line

To avoid confusion among customers and clerks, most retailers buy

© 1979 by Houghton Mifflin Company

(continued)

**Figure 12-4
Retail Store Price
Line for Dresses**

$9.95 $12.95 $15.95 $19.95 $24.95 $29.95

△ goods on the basis of a ***price line*** (see Figure 12-4). The retailer specifies a range of prices to be charged for a given kind of product. The owner of a retail dress shop, for example, may use $9.95, $12.95, $15.95, $19.95, $24.95, and $29.95 as standard selling prices, buying and stocking only dresses that qualify for these prices. Producers, in turn, recognize traditional pricing and act accordingly.

The price points that a retailer selects are significant. By experience the retailer determines the top, bottom, and intermediate points on the price line. Prices that are too low or too high will result in fewer sales and more inventory. Retailers must judge price steps in the light of consumers' expectations. A consumer interested in spending $12.95 for a dress might purchase one for $9.95 or $15.95. If the intervals on the price line are too great, there may be overwhelming resistance to the price.

Most shoppers have a price range in mind. The range often depends on some anchor point of judgment based on advertising or earlier shopping. The limits of the range depend on the anchor point. The lower this point is, the narrower will be the range; the higher the anchor point is, the wider the acceptable price range will be. Whether consumers know specifically about price lines or not, they do know approximately what prices to expect from the stores where they prefer to shop. Price lines simplify buying for both the consumer and the store.

© 1979 by Houghton Mifflin Company

Exercise 2

Context and Textbooks

Select a textbook you are studying in a college course and use it to find the meanings of ten words that are explained in the context of the book. Write the title and author of the textbook on the following lines:

Title: _____

Author: _____

Use headings and words printed in special type to help you find words explained in the textbook. Write the words and their meanings in the spaces below.

WRITE WORDS HERE: WRITE MEANINGS HERE:

1. _____   _____

    _____   _____

                   _____

                   _____

2. _____   _____

    _____   _____

                   _____

                   _____

3. _____   _____

    _____   _____

                   _____

                   _____

4. _____   _____

    _____   _____

                   _____

                   _____

(continued)

5. _____   _____

   _____   _____

                      _____

                      _____

6. _____   _____

   _____   _____

                      _____

                      _____

7. _____   _____

   _____   _____

                      _____

                      _____

8. _____   _____

   _____   _____

                      _____

                      _____

9. _____   _____

   _____   _____

                      _____

                      _____

10. _____   _____

    _____   _____

                      _____

                      _____

© 1979 by Houghton Mifflin Company

Chapter 4   Finding Word Meanings in Pictures

Just as the meanings of words can be revealed in the context of sentences and longer passages, they can also often be found in the context of pictures. To understand this statement, underline the correct answer to the following question:

Which of the following is neither *concave* nor *convex?*
    a. the outside of a basketball
    b. the inside of a basketball
    c. the outside of the earth
    d. the inside of the earth

You should have noticed your eyes wanting to study the following picture for the answer to the question:

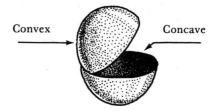

When you examine this picture, you can determine that the correct answer to the question is "the inside of the earth," because you can see that the outside of any sphere is convex and that the inside of a *hollow* sphere only is concave. Since the inside of the earth is not hollow, it is not concave.

Illustrations and pictures serve many different purposes. For one thing, they can make a book or magazine more appealing to the eye and therefore more likely to be purchased. Very often, though, readers assume that pictures are in books only to decorate them; thus, they fail to study pictures for the vast amounts of information they sometimes give. The purpose of this chapter is to help you understand how helpful pictures can be in giving information about the meanings of words so you will develop the habit of studying them for the information they often contain.

This chapter is arranged in three "steps"; *you will profit from it most if you do the steps in the order in which they are presented.*

© 1979 by Houghton Mifflin Company

STEP 1: PRETEST

On the following pages you will find five pictures you can use to determine the meanings of some words that appear in college textbooks. In order to understand how helpful the pictures are for finding word meanings, try to answer the following multiple-choice questions *before* you look at the pictures. You will have another opportunity to answer the questions again after you study the pictures.

Underline as many correct answers as you can:

1. In the *Herring illusion*
   a. two straight lines appear to be curved.
   b. two curved lines appear to be straight.
   c. a perfect circle is distorted in shape.
   d. a perfect square is distorted in shape.

2. *Megalopoli* are large
   a. countries.
   b. cities.
   c. deserts.
   d. rivers.

3. *Market segmentation* refers to
   a. types of merchandise sold by various stores.
   b. sources of merchandise sold by various stores.
   c. consumers who switch from one product to another.
   d. consumers who will and will not buy a product.

4. *Channels of distribution* refers to
   a. the route of a product from producer to consumer.
   b. shipment of products by truck, rail, ship, and air.
   c. the types of stores that distribute a product.
   d. depth of penetration into various marketplaces.

5. The *hydrologic cycle* refers to a pattern of the distribution of
   a. intelligence.
   b. health.
   c. money.
   d. water.

STEP 2: CONTEXT AND PICTURES

Now that you have done Step 1, study each of the following pictures to answer the question that appears below it. Underline the correct answers:

The Herring Illusion

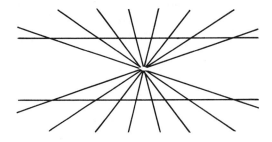

1. In the *Herring illusion*
   - a. two straight lines appear to be curved.
   - b. two curved lines appear to be straight.
   - c. a perfect circle is distorted in shape.
   - d. a perfect square is distorted in shape.

Possible Future Megalopoli in the United States of America

© 1979 by Houghton Mifflin Company

2. *Megalopoli* are large
      a. countries.
      b. cities.
      c. deserts.
      d. rivers.

Market Segmentation of College Students Located Within 400 Miles of a Ski Resort[1]

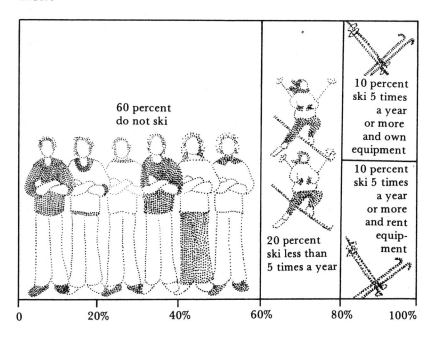

3. *Market segmentation* refers to
      a. types of merchandise sold by various stores.
      b. sources of merchandise sold by various stores.
      c. consumers who switch from one product to another.
      d. consumers who will and will not buy a product.

[1] Redrawn from MODERN BUSINESS, 2nd edition, by S. B. Rosenblatt, R. L. Bonnington, and B. E. Needles, Jr. Copyright © 1977 by Houghton Mifflin Company. Used by permission.

Four Channels of Distribution[2]

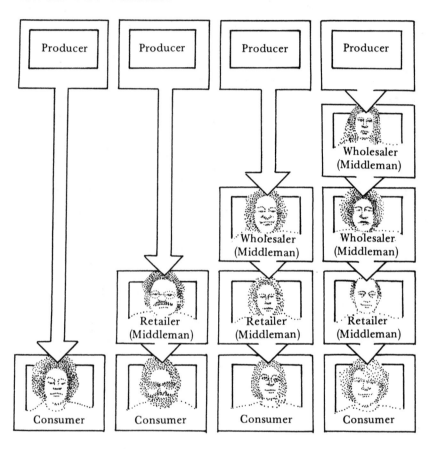

4. *Channels of distribution* refers to

      a. the route of a product from producer to consumer.

      b. shipment of products by truck, rail, ship, and air.

      c. the types of stores that distribute a product.

      d. depth of penetration into various marketplaces.

[2] Redrawn from MODERN BUSINESS, 2nd edition, by S. B. Rosenblatt, R. L. Bonnington, and B. E. Needles, Jr. Copyright © 1977 by Houghton Mifflin Company. Used by permission.

© 1979 by Houghton Mifflin Company

The Hydrologic Cycle[3]

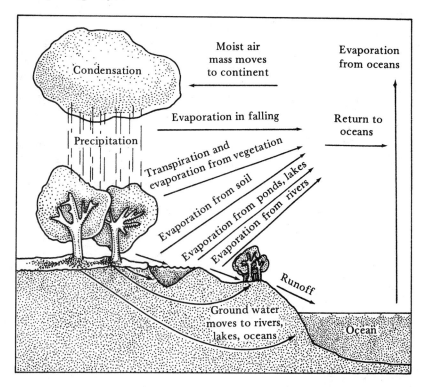

5. The *hydrologic cycle* refers to a pattern of the distribution of
   a. intelligence.
   b. health.
   c. money.
   d. water.

[3]Redrawn from BETWEEN TWO WORLDS: A NEW INTRODUCTION TO GEOG-
RAPHY, by Robert A. Harper and Theodore H. Schmudde. Copyright © 1973 by
Houghton Mifflin Company. Used by permission.

**STEP 3: EVALUATE
WHAT YOU LEARNED**

The correct answers to the questions are given in the answer key. Count 20 points for each correct answer in Steps 1 and 2:

1. What was your score for Step 1? _____

2. What was your score for Step 2? _____

3. By how much did your score increase from Step 1 to Step 2? _____

Illustrations, pictures, and other graphic materials do not always help in understanding the meanings of words; however, from what you practiced in this chapter check if you believe pictures *can* be

_____ extremely helpful for finding word meanings.

_____ very useful to study for word meanings.

_____ a little helpful for finding word meanings.

_____ not very helpful for finding word meanings.

Also, check if in the future you believe you will study pictures for word meanings

_____ all of the time.

_____ most of the time.

_____ once in a while.

_____ seldom.

© 1979 by Houghton Mifflin Company

SECTION 2   FINDING WORD MEANINGS IN WORD STRUCTURE

In Chapters 2, 3, and 4 you learned how to use sentences, longer passages, and pictures to find the meanings of words without consulting a dictionary or other reference source. The purpose of the five chapters in this section of the book is also to help you find word meanings without referring to a dictionary.

Chapters 5, 6, 7, and 8 explain how to find the meanings of a type of words called *derivatives*. These are words that contain an English base word and a prefix or suffix. *Unkind, kindness,* and *unkindness* are examples of derivatives. *Unkind* contains a prefix and a base word; *kindness* contains a base word and a suffix; and *unkindness* contains a prefix, base word, and suffix. It is estimated that more than one in every three words that are new to you in your college study will be derivatives. Most of them will be much more difficult to analyze than *unkind, kindness,* and *unkindness;* the things you learn in Chapters 5 through 8 will help you become more expert at finding the meanings of derivatives without referring to a dictionary.

Also, in *Chapter 9* you will learn to find the meanings of words that contain combining forms. *Combining forms* are Latin and Greek word parts such as the *biblio-* and *-phile* in our word *bibliophile. Bibliophile* is defined to mean "one who has a love for books." Its meaning is closely related to the meaning of *biblio-,* which is "book," and the meaning of *-phile,* which is "having a love for." Chapter 9 explains how you can use combining forms to find and learn the meanings of many interesting and unusual words.

Chapter 5   Prefixes

Prefixes are word parts that are added to the beginnings of base words to form new words, called *derivatives*. For example:

PREFIX		BASE WORD		DERIVATIVE
re-	+	write	=	rewrite
un-	+	clear	=	unclear
non-	+	standard	=	nonstandard
in-	+	complete	=	incomplete
dis-	+	agree	=	disagree

If you examine a large unabridged dictionary in your college library, you will find thousands of words that begin with *re-, un-, non-, in-, dis-*, and other prefixes.

DO YOU KNOW THE MEANINGS OF PREFIXES?

If you know the meanings of prefixes, you can use them to figure out the meanings of words. For example, if you know that the prefix *pseudo-* means "false," you can figure out the meaning of *pseudoscience*, which is "false science."

In this chapter you will review the meanings of the most common prefixes and learn the meanings of some important prefixes that you do not already know. The prefixes in the following list are among the most common ones—you should know the meanings of *all* of them. Quiz yourself to see how many you can define correctly. In the example, *re-* is defined to mean "again." Write the meanings of other prefixes:

© 1979 by Houghton Mifflin Company

Example. *re-*, as in *rewrite*

_____ *again* _____

1. *post-*, as in *postwar*

_____

2. *dis-*, as in *disconnect*

_____

3. *un-*, as in *unlock*

_____

4. *inter-*, as in *intermarriage*

_____

5. *trans-*, as in *trans-Sahara*

_____

6. *pre-*, as in *premarriage*

_____

Check your answers by studying the meanings of prefixes listed on page 48. If you were not able to give the correct meanings of some of these prefixes, you will have learned their meanings by the time you complete the exercises for this chapter. If you knew the meanings of most of the prefixes, the exercises for this chapter will help you become more skillful at finding the meanings of derivatives that contain prefixes.

LEARNING THE MEANINGS OF PREFIXES

On page 48 you will find a list of the most important prefixes and their meanings. All of the meanings of prefixes in the list entitled "Most Useful Meanings of Prefixes" have been carefully selected to be as useful as possible to you when you use them to determine the meanings of derivatives. It is strongly urged that you learn the meaning of any prefix you do not already know.

As you study the prefixes and their meanings, notice that the prefix *un-* has more than one meaning. Also notice that the prefix

Most Useful Meanings of Prefixes

PREFIX	MEANING(S)	EXAMPLE
1. un-	not	*un*happy; not happy
	do the opposite	*un*lock; do the opposite of lock
	remove	*un*chain; remove the chain
2. non-	not	*non*living; not living
3. in-	not	*in*direct; not direct
im-	not	*im*perfect; not perfect
		*im*measurable; not measurable
il-	not	*il*legal; not legal
ir-	not	*ir*regular; not regular
4. dis-	opposite of	*dis*appear; vanish
5. mis-	wrongly, badly, incorrectly	*mis*spell; spell wrongly, badly, or incorrectly
6. mal-	wrongly, badly	*mal*functioning; functioning wrongly or badly
7. pre-	before	*pre*war; before a war
8. post-	after	*post*war; after a war
9. inter-	between	*inter*state; between states
10. trans-	across	*trans*atlantic; across the Atlantic
11. pro-	favoring, for	*pro*war; favoring war
12. anti-	opposing, against	*anti*war; against war
13. hyper-	exceedingly	*hyper*active; exceedingly active
14. re-	again	*re*write; write again
15. pseudo-	false	*pseudo*science; false science
16. ex-	former	*ex*-president; former president
17. semi-	partly	*semi*public; partly public

© 1979 by Houghton Mifflin Company

in- is spelled *im-* before words beginning with *m* or *p; il-* before words beginning with *l;* and *ir-* before words beginning with *r.* These spelling differences came about as a result of pronunciation— it is easier to say *il*legal than *in*legal or *im*measurable than *in*measurable.

DEFINING WORDS THAT CONTAIN PREFIXES

Usually it is not helpful to define word using the word that is being defined. For example, you would not define *beverage* by saying "a beverage is a beverage." Rather, you would say something such as "a beverage is a liquid that people drink."

However, when a word is made by adding a prefix to a base word, the base word is often used in its definition. Thus, it is correct to say that *unclear* means "not clear" and *unimpeachable* means "not impeachable." Even dictionary writers use this procedure. Notice that one definition of *rewrite* uses the base word:

> **re·write** (rē-rīt') *tr.v.* **-wrote** (-rōt'), **-written** (-rit'n), **-writing, -writes. 1.** To write again, especially in a different form. **2.** *Journalism.* To write (an account given by a reporter) in a form suitable for publishing. —*n.* (rē'rīt'). An article so written. —**re·writ'er** *n.*

You may use this same method of defining words when words are made by adding a prefix to the beginning of a base word.

PRACTICE PROBLEMS

The problems for this chapter should increase your ability to find the correct meanings of words that contain prefixes and base words. *Solve the problems by rewriting the words printed in dark type so the prefix is removed and the phrase you write can be used to replace the word or phrase printed in dark type.* Following are sample problems that have been solved and an explanation of how they were solved:

1. We wanted to enjoy the scenery on the way to Philadelphia, so we took **an indirect route.**

a route that was not direct

2. The **ex-president** will officiate at the ceremony for the new officers.

former president

3. After the accident, he had to **relearn how to walk and talk**.

learn how to walk and talk again

Notice that the words printed in dark type in the sentences have been rewritten without the prefix and in such a way that they may be removed from the sentences and replaced with the rewritten version:

1. We wanted to enjoy the scenery on the way to Philadelphia, so we took **a route that was not direct**.
2. The **former president** will officiate at the ceremony for the new officers.
3. After the accident, he had to **learn how to walk and talk again**.

© 1979 by Houghton Mifflin Company

Exercise 1   *Prefixes*

The directions for solving these problems are given under "Practice Problems."

1. Please **unknot** this string for me.

2. We respect **incorruptible judges.**

3. The snowstorm made the mountain road **impassable.**

4. The works of eighteenth-century artists are **irreplaceable** if destroyed.

5. It is **illogical** to assume you will live forever.

6. "Men, **dismount** your horses and draw your swords."

7. If you form opinions of people the first time you meet them, you may **misjudge them.**

8. **Nonmembers** are not allowed to vote on matters that pertain to members only.

9. Dental work to correct a **malformation** of the teeth is usually quite expensive.

10. This ham has been **precooked,** so you may eat it without further preparation.

(continued)

11. The patient will receive two days of special **postoperative care** before being sent home.

_____

12. The flight from America to France is an **intercontinental trip.**

_____

13. We made the **transcontinental trip** from New York to San Francisco by car in just over four days.

_____

14. Ten members of the jury were **proconviction,** but the other two held out for acquittal.

_____

15. Communist countries still tend to be **anticapitalist,** even though they are increasing their use of capitalistic methods.

_____

© 1979 by Houghton Mifflin Company

Exercise 2   *Prefixes*

The directions for solving these problems are given just before the first exercise for this chapter.

1. This small boat is not suitable for **transoceanic trips.**

_____

2. Every day thousands of people in this world die of **malnutrition.**

_____

3. Some people should not be given Novocain because they are **hypersensitive** to it.

_____

4. Maybe the machine will work if you **reinsert the quarter.**

_____

5. The devilish child wore a **pseudoangelic** smile.

_____

6. Ellen is going to remarry her **ex-husband.**

_____

7. Leave the door **semiopen** so the cat can get in.

_____

8. They **prerecorded the television show** so it could be shown at any convenient time.

_____

9. Some **profaculty students** gathered outside the Administration Building to protest the dismissal of two professors.

_____

10. **Antiliquor forces** worked to see that no alcoholic beverages would be sold in the community.

_____

(*continued*)

11. People were sunbathing **seminude** on the beach.

_____

12. My **ex-teacher** and her husband opened a travel agency.

_____

13. **Unleash** the dog and let him run around in the yard.

_____

14. Our football team is going to play a **postseason exhibition game.**

_____

15. A company is not likely to **rehire an employee** who was fired for doing poor work.

_____

© 1979 by Houghton Mifflin Company

Exercise 3

Prefixes

The directions for solving these problems are given just before the first exercise for this chapter.

1. The Boy Scouts and the Girl Scouts are **nonprofit organizations.**

2. She did poorly on the test because she **misinterpreted too many questions.**

3. His stomach pain was a **pseudoappendicitis attack.**

4. They are engaged in **illegitimate business activities.**

5. **I miscounted my money** and now realize I have ten dollars more than I thought I had.

6. We took the **nonstop flight** to Chicago.

7. Avoid interrupting your teachers with **irrelevant questions** while they are lecturing.

8. Chewing gum is **indigestible.**

9. Nancy was **immovable** in her decision that she would graduate from college.

(*continued*)

10. **International relations** must improve if we are to have peace in this century.

_____

11. This product is used for **disinfecting** the bathroom.

_____

12. The doctor was shocked at the **hyperbrutal** treatment the child had received from his parents.

_____

13. It once seemed that the potential of humankind was **illimitable**.

_____

14. When wars are over, many **ex-soldiers** have difficulty finding employment.

_____

15. You'll need to **unzip** your jacket before you can take it off.

_____

© 1979 by Houghton Mifflin Company

Exercise 4   *Prefixes*

The directions for solving these problems are given just before the first exercise for this chapter.

1. President Truman had the habit of taking a **postbreakfast walk.**

_____

2. I must **reinsist** that knowing the meanings of prefixes will help you find the meanings of many words.

_____

3. The **pseudobiographical** format is often effective in novels.

_____

4. The Pope recently took a strong **antidivorce stand.**

_____

5. In noisy cities, apartments are at best only **semipeaceful.**

_____

6. The doctor faced a **malpractice suit** for doing an operation that did not need to be done.

_____

7. Some colleges admit only students who they can **predetermine** will be good students.

_____

8. This community is **proeducation** and pays high taxes to support the best possible schools.

_____

9. Homemade apple pie is **irresistible.**

_____

(continued)

10. Speech therapists can help some people correct **indistinct speech.**

_____

11. The students were **hypercritical** of the school's decision to raise the cost of tuition.

_____

12. The distances of outer space are **immeasurable.**

_____

13. The police **disarmed** the thief and put him in handcuffs.

_____

14. There is no need to stamp that letter; you can send it through the **interdepartmental mail.**

_____

15. We dressed warmly for our **trans-Siberian train trip.**

_____

© 1979 by Houghton Mifflin Company

Chapter 6 Base Words

When you study the structure of derivatives to find their meanings, you will always need to locate the base words they contain. Derivatives do not always contain a prefix and they do not always contain a suffix, but they always contain a base word. This chapter explains why base words are not always easy to find and gives you practice so you may become more accurate in finding the base words in derivatives.

FIVE HINTS ON FINDING BASE WORDS

Look for Meaning, Not for Spelling Alone. Spelling can help you find base words in derivatives, but it can also lead you to select an incorrect base word. You must always answer this question about the base word you select for a derivative: *Does the base word I have selected have a meaning that is closely related to the meaning of the derivative?* If the answer is "no," you should search for another base word. This is illustrated below using the derivative *discussible:*

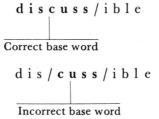

Discuss, not *cuss,* is the base word in *discussible. Discuss* means "to talk over"; *cuss,* which means "to curse," is not closely related to the meaning of *discussible. Discussible* means "that which can be used as the basis for a serious conversation."

Always Look for the "Smallest" Base Word. When you look for base words in derivatives, always look for the smallest base word that is closely related to the meaning of the derivative. This is illustrated with the derivative *reclaimable:*

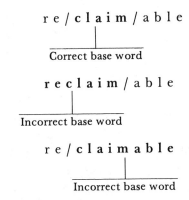

Reclaim and *claimable* are not the base words in *reclaimable;* they are themselves derivatives of the base word *claim.* The base word in *reclaimable* is *claim.*

Sometimes *e*'s Are Dropped from Base Words. Very often when base words end in the letter *e,* the *e*'s are dropped before suffixes that begin with vowels are added. When *e*'s are dropped from base words, they must be replaced. For example, the *e* was dropped from *mature* to form the derivative *immaturity:*

$$i\ m\ /\ m\ a\ t\ u\ r\ /\ i\ t\ y$$

The base word in *immaturity* is *mature,* not *matur.*

Sometimes *y*'s in Base Words Are Changed to *i*'s. Many times when base words end in *y,* the *y*'s are changed to *i*'s before suffixes are added. When you find a derivative in which *y* has been changed to *i,* you must change the *i* back to *y* to find the correct base word. For example, the *y* in *certify* was changed to *i* to form the derivative *certification:*

© 1979 by Houghton Mifflin Company

certifi / c a t i o n

The base word in *certification* is *certify*, not *certifi*.

Sometimes Base Words Undergo Other Spelling Changes. There are many other spelling changes base words may undergo when suffixes are added to them. It would be impractical to list all the possible spelling changes, but the following list will give you some idea of the kinds of spelling changes you should look for:

BASE WORD	DERIVATIVE	UNUSUAL SPELLING CHANGE
reclaim	reclamation	*i* in recla*i*m is dropped
pregnant	pregnancy	*t* in pregnan*t* is dropped
decide	decision	*d* in deci*d*e is changed to *s*
provoke	provocation	*k* in provo*k*e is changed to *c*
repeat	repetition	*a* in repe*a*t is dropped
recognize	recognition	*z* in recogni*z*e is dropped

These spelling changes in base words are given as examples only, and you do not need to learn them. However, when you search for base words in derivatives, you should keep in mind that base words can undergo many different types of spelling changes.

PRACTICE PROBLEMS

The practice problems will help you become more skillful at finding base words in derivatives. When you look for base words, remember that (1) the meaning of the base word you select must be closely related to the meaning of the derivative, and (2) you should always look for the "smallest" base words. *Solve the following problems by writing the base words in the derivatives and then by writing*

1. "no change" if there is no change of spelling in the base word
2. "*e* dropped" if a final *e* was dropped from the base word
3. "*y* to *i*" if a final *y* in the base word was changed to *i*
4. "other change" if there was a spelling change in the base word other than the dropping of a final *e* or the changing of a *y* to an *i*

Following are examples of how the problems are solved:

1. irreducibility _reduce_ — e dropped
2. untruthfulness _truth_ — no change
3. intelligence _intelligent_ — other change
4. colonization _colony_ — y to i

© 1979 by Houghton Mifflin Company

Exercise 1

Base Words

The directions for solving these problems are given under "Practice Problems."

1. redistribute _____

2. frustration _____

3. misalliance _____

4. interdependent _____

5. angular _____

6. retention _____

7. unrecognizable _____

8. harmonious _____

9. unimprovable _____

10. nonconformity _____

11. disposable _____

12. plentiful _____

13. guiltiness _____

14. description _____

15. fabulous _____

16. merciless _____

17. indisputable _____

18. reverification _____

19. combatant _____

20. scientific _____

© 1979 by Houghton Mifflin Company

Exercise 2

Base Words

The directions for solving these problems are given just before the first exercise for this chapter.

1. decency   _____

2. immeasurable   _____

3. disinterestedness   _____

4. unfeminine   _____

5. tabular   _____

6. disqualification   _____

7. dentistry   _____

8. custodian   _____

9. indefinable   _____

10. disagreeable   _____

11. mispronounce   _____

12. incomparable   _____

13. defiance   _____

14. ceremonial   _____

15. discontinuousness   _____

16. unionization   _____

17. recertification   _____

18. predetermination   _____

19. thriftiness   _____

20. evasion   _____

© 1979 by Houghton Mifflin Company

Exercise 3   *Base Words*

The directions for solving these problems are given just before the first exercise for this chapter.

1. unreliable   _____
2. invariably   _____
3. vacancy   _____
4. redistribution   _____
5. illogical   _____
6. invasion   _____
7. decomposition   _____
8. indistinguishable _____
9. intervention   _____
10. effortlessly   _____
11. miscalculation   _____
12. sobriety   _____
13. overexposure   _____
14. miraculous   _____
15. penniless   _____
16. unenviable   _____
17. postponement   _____
18. irreversible   _____
19. possibility   _____
20. luxurious   _____

© 1979 by Houghton Mifflin Company

Chapter 7   Suffixes

At least one-third of all English words end with suffixes. As the difficulty of reading material increases, so does the number of words with suffixes. It is very likely that at least one out of every three new words you encounter in your college study will contain a suffix, so the ability to find the meanings of derivatives that contain suffixes is essential to you if you wish to expand your vocabulary or find the meanings of words without consulting a dictionary.

SUFFIXES AND THE MEANINGS OF WORDS

There is a strong relationship between the meaning of a prefix and the meaning of a derivative that contains a prefix. *Re-* added to a base word usually means "again," *mal-* added to a base word usually means "bad," and so on. Suffixes, on the other hand, do not usually add any *specific* meanings when they are added to base words.

Even the most familiar suffixes have many different meanings. Edward L. Thorndike studied the meanings of suffixes and found, for example, that the suffix *-ful,* as in *helpful,* has a total of 39 meanings and that the suffix *-er,* as in *singer,* has a total of 167 meanings.*

Fortunately, the wide range of meanings for each suffix does not present much difficulty because it is usually possible to find the

*Edward L. Thorndike, *The Teaching of English Suffixes* (New York: Teachers College Press, 1941).

meanings of derivatives without knowing the meanings of suffixes. For example, it is not necessary to know the meaning of *-ity* to find the meaning of *particularity* in this sentence:

John's **particularity** is evident in the way he dresses.

The base word in *particularity* can be used to understand John—John is *particular*. Similarly, it is not necessary to know the meaning of *-arily* to find the meaning of *momentarily* in this context:

The doctor will arrive **momentarily**.

The base word in *momentarily* may be used to understand when the doctor will arrive—in a *moment*.

There is, then, one important principle to keep in mind when you try to determine the meanings of derivatives that contain suffixes:

Use the meanings of base words to find the meanings of derivatives in the contexts in which they appear.

It is because of this principle that Chapter 6 was devoted exclusively to helping you refine your ability to find base words in derivatives.

PRACTICE PROBLEMS

Some people become confused when they see a word in a form in which they have never seen it before—they "freeze" and assume that if they have never seen the word, they do not know what it means. One of the major purposes of the following exercises is to help you understand that if you know a base word, you should be comfortable with derivatives of it. For example, if you know the word *participate*, you should be comfortable with *participatory*, even though you may never have seen that word before.

Each problem consists of three words (a verb, a noun, and an adjective) and a sentence with two blank spaces. You are to use two of the words to complete the sentences, as shown in this example:

© 1979 by Houghton Mifflin Company

regulate, regulation, regulatory

We need to ___*regulate*___ imports so they do not adversely affect our economy, and that is the purpose of our ___*regulatory*___ laws regarding imports.

You should not find these problems difficult to do; but if you have more than three incorrect solutions in any set of exercises, you should study your incorrect solutions with the use of a dictionary.

© 1979 by Houghton Mifflin Company

Exercise 1

Suffixes

The directions for solving these problems are given under "Practice Problems."

1. *digest, digestion, digestive*

I find mushrooms and onions difficult to _____;

my _____ system does not handle them well.

2. *distract, distraction, distractible*

Children are often exceedingly _____; a fly on

the ceiling will _____ my little boy.

3. *evolve, evolution, evolutionary*

It is our own efforts more than an _____

process that help us to _____ to the people

we want to be.

4. *legalize, legality, legal*

I am concerned with what is right, not with what is merely

_____; morality interests me much more than

_____.

5. *manage, management, managerial*

All our positions in _____ require previous

_____ experience.

6. *manipulate, manipulation, manipulative*

He is not easy to _____, but he is more likely

to respond to _____ by women than by men.

7. *dramatize, drama, dramatic*

It is difficult to _____ the creative process of

painting because painting is not _____.

(*continued*)

8. *duplicate, duplication, duplicative*

Since you have only a few pages to _____, I suggest that the _____ be done on a photo-copying machine.

9. *popularize, popularity, popular*

Soccer will enjoy greater _____ when there is more advertising to _____ it.

10. *presume, presumption, presumptuous*

Your _____ is incorrect; you may _____ what you want, but I will not tell you my age.

11. *persuade, persuasion, persuasive*

She is very _____. I think she could _____ me to do just about anything.

12. *emphasize, emphasis, emphatic*

When we were young, we were _____ in stating our dislikes; now we _____ what we like.

13. *enforce, enforcement, enforceable*

When laws are not _____, little money is spent on their _____.

14. *rehabilitate, rehabilitation, rehabilitative*

Criminals need _____, but we have not devised good ways to _____ them.

15. *erupt, eruption, eruptive*

If the discontent of the people should _____, the _____ will lead to a bloody revolution in that country.

© 1979 by Houghton Mifflin Company

Exercise 2   _Suffixes_

The directions for solving these problems are given just before the
first exercise for this chapter.

1. _predict, prediction, predictable_

It is difficult to _____ the weather because

weather is not very _____ .

2. _experiment, experimentation, experimental_

Science uses _____ . _____

studies expand our knowledge.

3. _exploit, exploitation, exploitative_

Some businesses _____ the poor. One form of

_____ is high interest rates on loans.

4. _argue, argument, argumentative_

I do not enjoy an _____ , so I try to avoid

_____ people.

5. _analyze, analysis, analytical_

Various _____ tools are used to _____

the causes of deviant behavior.

6. _attain, attainment, attainable_

Perfection is not _____ , but we can all

_____ greater perfection than we now have.

7. _formalize, formality, formal_

They are not _____ people, but they want the

_____ of a church wedding.

8. _economize, economy, economical_

If you eat fresh fruit when it is most _____ ,

(_continued_)

you will not only ——————————————— but you will also en-

joy the fruit at its best.

9. *harmonize, harmony, harmonious*

Brown and blue are ——————————————— in nature, so they

should ——————————————— in your living room.

10. *hesitate, hesitancy, hesitatingly*

Try not to ———————————————; ——————————————— will

make you appear to be uncertain.

11. *mechanize, mechanism, mechanically*

There is a ——————————————— for most kitchen chores—

cooking can now be done ———————————————.

12. *meditate, meditation, meditative*

There seems to be value in ———————————————; people who

——————————————— report increased happiness.

13. *minister, ministration, ministerial*

Nurses ——————————————— to the sick, and most of them

place a high value on the ——————————————— aspect of their

work.

14. *conclude, conclusion, conclusive*

You ——————————————— I will marry you, but your think-

ing on this issue is not ———————————————.

15. *rely, reliability, reliable*

We are interested in your ——————————————— because we

need ——————————————— workers.

© 1979 by Houghton Mifflin Company

Exercise 3

Suffixes

The directions for solving these problems are given just before the first exercise for this chapter.

1. *observe, observation, observant*

I didn't _____ where she went. Ask Fred; he's

more _____ of where she goes than I am.

2. *mystify, mystery, mysterious*

These statistics should not _____ you; there is

nothing _____ about percentages.

3. *prevent, prevention, preventable*

We need to work for fire _____ even though

many fires are not _____.

4. *obligate, obligation, obligatory*

The bill is not your _____—you did not

_____ yourself to take me to lunch.

5. *philosophize, philosophy, philosophically*

She loves _____ and can _____

on most any subject for hours.

6. *generalize, generalization, general*

When you _____, you can be certain your

_____ will not apply in every case.

7. *edify, edification, edifying*

My parents tried to _____ me by having me

read the classics, but I was not ready for _____.

(*continued*)

8. *equalize, equality, equal*

We believe all people are created _____, but we

have not found how to give _____ to all.

9. *compare, comparison, comparative*

I cannot _____ the two jobs—I find no

_____ between them.

10. *compensate, compensation, compensatory*

We will _____ you for your extra work; expect

_____ pay in your next check.

11. *dominate, domination, dominant*

He is a very _____ person; his whole family is

suppressed by his _____.

12. *contemplate, contemplation, contemplative*

If you are _____, you will find that the moun-

tains are conducive to _____.

13. *defy, defiance, defiant*

I would not _____ a police officer to give me a

ticket for going through a red light; I think few people would be

_____ under those circumstances.

14. *describe, description, descriptive*

Don't skip the _____ passages; _____

is the best part of that book.

15. *disagree, disagreement, disagreeable*

If you like to _____, it is always possible to

find a point of _____.

© 1979 by Houghton Mifflin Company

Chapter 8   Finding Word Meanings from Word Structure and Context

In Chapters 2 through 7 you learned the two basic ways to find the meanings of words without referring to a dictionary: (1) looking for meanings in context and (2) looking for meanings in word structure. This chapter contains some problems that will help you understand how you should use these skills together to find the meanings of words in the material you read in college.

The problems consist of passages in which some words are printed in dark type. Solve the problems by

1. reading a passage,
2. deciding if the meanings of the words printed in dark type in a passage may be found from (a) context, (b) word structure, or (c) both context and word structure, and
3. writing the meanings of the words printed in dark type.

Following is a sample problem, its solution, and a discussion of how it was solved:

> Britain once had control over many countries, but she no longer has this **imperial**₁ power. This reminds us of the **impermanence**₂ of global influence; it, like everything else, comes to an end. The lessons of history remind us that it is **indisputable**₃ that the leading world powers in the future will not be those we know today.

1. imperial   context ✓   word structure

having control over other countries

2. impermanence   context ✓   word structure ✓

lack of permanence — will come to an end

3. indisputable   context   word structure ✓

not able to be disputed

Following is an explanation of how the problems were solved:

1. For *imperial,* a check (√) is placed next to "context" because the meaning of the word may be gotten only from context: "had control over many countries."

2. For *impermanence,* a check (√) is placed next to "context" *and* "word structure" because the meaning of the word is revealed in context by the words "comes to an end" and also in word structure; *impermanence = not + permanence,* or "lack of permanence."

3. For *indisputable,* a check (√) is placed next to "word structure" because the meaning of the word may be gotten only from word structure: *indisputable = not + dispute + able,* or "not able to be disputed."

Solve the problems in the exercises that follow in the same way, so that you may better understand how you may use both context and word structure to find the meanings of words without referring to a dictionary.

© 1979 by Houghton Mifflin Company

Exercise 1   *Word Structure and Context*

The directions for solving these problems are given just before this exercise.

PRETENSION, JARGON, AND CLICHÉ

Pretension, jargon, and cliché are roadblocks to good communication.

When writers select words for the purpose of impressing readers rather than to express thoughts clearly, we say they use **pretension₁**. Some writers never use a familiar word when they can use an unfamiliar one; they write "**inebriated₂**" for *drunk,* "**perambulate₃**" for *walk,* and "interred" for *buried.*

Jargon₄ is somewhat like pretension, but it differs in that its purpose seems to be for **obscuring₅**, or clouding, meaning. Also sometimes called **gobbledygook₆**, jargon is used when a military officer refers to bombs as "**antipersonnel₇** detonating devices," an economist calls poor financial policies "**inoperative₈** fiscal procedures," or a sociologist speaks of poor families as "**familial₉** entities of the lower economic strata."

A **cliché₁₀** is a phrase that has been used so many times it has become **trite₁₁**—worn out, tired. Phrases such as "blushing bride," "clear as day," and "quick as a flash" have all been heard so often that they are, **undeniably₁₂**, clichés. Clichés block communication because they give readers the impression that writers did not try hard enough to express thoughts in their own words.

You, of course, should avoid pretension, jargon, and cliché in your writing.

1. **pretension**   context   word structure

_____

2. **inebriated**   context   word structure

_____

3. **perambulate**   context   word structure

_____

(continued)

4. jargon   context   word structure

_____

5. obscuring   context   word structure

_____

6. gobbledygook   context   word structure

_____

7. antipersonnel   context   word structure

_____

8. inoperative   context   word structure

_____

9. familial   context   word structure

_____

10. cliché   context   word structure

_____

11. trite   context   word structure

_____

12. undeniably   context   word structure

_____

© 1979 by Houghton Mifflin Company

Exercise 2   *Word Structure and Context*

The directions for solving these problems are given just before the first exercise for this chapter.

FORMAL, INFORMAL, AND SLANG USAGES

Many **grammarians**[1] believe there are some words that should be **disallowed**[2] in serious writing. They distinguish among formal, **informal**[3], and slang meanings for words and discourage students from using any but formal meanings when writing serious papers.

Since most definitions are **formal**[4] (may be used in serious writing), dictionaries usually include distinguishing labels only when meanings are considered informal or slang. Meanings in dictionaries are labeled "**slang**[5]" when they are believed to be the type that should not be used in either serious speech or serious writing. For example, dictionaries warn that "**kook**[6]," "weirdo," and "nut" are slang when used to refer to an **unpredictable**[7] person.

Lexicographers[8] label meanings "informal" or "**colloquial**[9]" when, in their opinion, these meanings are appropriately used in speech or in letters to friends, but not in serious papers. For example, the meaning "certainly" for the word *sure* is labeled "informal" in dictionaries to indicate that it should not be used this way in serious writing: "She sure is nice."

When you write serious papers for college, it would be **prudent**[10] to **scrutinize**[11] the words you use for any that may be **inconsistent**[12] with good usage. In serious writing it is always wise to examine carefully the words you use and to eliminate informal (or colloquial) and slang usages.

1. **grammarians**   context   word structure

_____

2. **disallowed**   context   word structure

_____

3. **informal**   context   word structure

_____

(continued)

4. formal   context   word structure

_____

5. slang   context   word structure

_____

6. kook   context   word structure

_____

7. unpredictable   context   word structure

_____

8. lexicographers context   word structure

_____

9. colloquial   context   word structure

_____

10. prudent   context   word structure

_____

11. scrutinize   context   word structure

_____

12. inconsistent   context   word structure

_____

© 1979 by Houghton Mifflin Company

Exercise 3   *Word Structure and Context*

The directions for solving these problems are given just before the first exercise for this chapter.

PLAGIARISM

Many college teachers read term papers carefully, **hypersensitive**[1] to the possibility that in every set of papers some students may be **culpable**[2] of the academic crime of copying the words of others and offering them as their own. Some students who copy what others wrote know this is **impermissible**[3], but others do not **apprehend**[4] the **inappropriateness**[5] of this act; they do not understand that it is wrong to **plagiarize**[6].

Whether the words of a writer are used **verbatim**[7] or whether they are **paraphrased**[8] (put in words other than those the writer used), they must be accompanied by a clear reference—a **citation**[9] in the form of a footnote. For example, the following words belong to a well-known authority on the writing of scholarly papers: "Failure to give credit in your papers for the loans made by other writers is plagiarism—a serious offense."[1] This footnoted quotation serves to **reinforce**[10] what has been said about the **inadvisability**[11] of plagiarizing, to demonstrate one way the exact words of writers may be shown, and to illustrate how **superscript**[12] numerals are used to direct readers' attention to footnotes at the bottoms of pages.

1. **hypersensitive**   context   word structure

2. **culpable**   context   word structure

3. **impermissible**   context   word structure

(*continued*)

[1] Kate L. Turabian, *Student's Guide for Writing College Papers,* 2nd ed. (Chicago: University of Chicago Press, 1969), p. 56.

4. apprehend　　　　context　　　　word structure

_____

5. inappropriateness　　　　context　　　　word structure

_____

6. plagiarize　　　　context　　　　word structure

_____

7. verbatim　　　　context　　　　word structure

_____

8. paraphrased　　　　context　　　　word structure

_____

9. citation　　　　context　　　　word structure

_____

10. reinforce　　　　context　　　　word structure

_____

11. inadvisability　　　　context　　　　word structure

_____

12. superscript　　　　context　　　　word structure

_____

© 1979 by Houghton Mifflin Company

Chapter 9 Combining Forms

Combining forms are word parts. But they are different from the prefixes and suffixes you have studied in this book, because they usually are not added to English base words; instead, words usually are created from combining forms when one combining form is joined to (or "combined" with) another.

WORDS MADE FROM COMBINING FORMS

Octagon is an example of a word made by joining two combining forms, octo- and -gon:

o c t a / g o n

Information about combining forms is given in dictionaries:

> **oc·ta·gon** (ŏk′tə-gŏn′) n. A polygon with eight sides and angles. [Latin octagōnum, from Greek oktagōnon, from neuter of oktagōnos, having eight angles : OCTO- + -GON.]

octo–, oct–. Indicates eight parts or elements; for example, **octopus, octameter, octane.** [Latin octō-, from octō, eight; Greek okta-, from oktō, eight. See oktō in Appendix.*]

–gon. Indicates a figure having a designated number of angles; for example, **nonagon.** [Greek -gōnon, from -gōnos, -angled, from gōnia, angle. See genu-¹ in Appendix.*]

The information "[octo- + -gon]" at the end of the entry for octagon is an example of the way dictionaries show that words are made from combining forms. The dictionary from which this entry was taken has separate, alphabetically listed entries for octo- and -gon. Octo- indicates "eight" and -gon indicates "a figure having a designated number of angles." An octagon is a figure having eight angles:

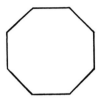

Neither *octo-* nor *-gon* is an English word, but both *octo-* and *-gon* have meanings that can be used to determine the meaning of English words in which they appear; they are examples of combining forms.

PRACTICE PROBLEMS

The problems for this chapter have been written so that you might understand that

1. combining forms are fairly consistent in their spellings, so you can find them when they appear in words,
2. combining forms are fairly consistent in their meanings, so you can use them to determine the meanings of words, and
3. combining forms can help you increase your vocabulary to include many interesting and unusual words.

Exercise 5 is especially important if you are studying a scientific or technical course.

© 1979 by Houghton Mifflin Company

Exercise 1

Mono-, Bi-, Tri-, etc.

Use the meanings of the combining forms in the following list to help you answer the multiple-choice questions in this exercise.

MEANING	COMBINING FORM	EXAMPLE
one	uni-	A _uni_cycle has one wheel.
	mono-	A _mono_cle is a glass for one eye.
two	bi-	A _bi_cycle has two wheels.
three	tri-	A _tri_cycle has three wheels.
four	quadr-	Four people sing in a _quadr_et.
five	quint-	Five people sing in a _quint_et.
six	sext-	Six people sing in a _sext_et.
seven	sept-	Seven people sing in a _sept_et.
eight	octo-	An _octo_pus has eight tentacles.
nine	nov-	_Nov_enas are nine days of prayer.
ten	deci-	The _deci_mal system uses units of 10.
	deca-	The _Deca_logue is the Ten Commandments.

Circle the letters in front of the correct answers.

1. In some countries people may have more than one marriage partner, but in this country one man is married to one woman. We practice
     a. polygamy.
     b. monogamy.
     c. bigamy.
     d. trigamy.

2. A biennial plant bears fruit every two years. Leap years are
     a. triennial.
     b. quadrennial.
     c. septennial.
     d. sexennial.

(continued)

3. Two people dropped out of the octet, so now it's a
    a. quintet.
    b. quartet.
    c. sextet.
    d. septet.

4. I do not expect to be here in the year 2076 to celebrate our country's
    a. centennial.
    b. bicentennial.
    c. tricentennial.
    d. quadricentennial.

5. In the ancient Roman calendar, the eighth month of the year was
    a. September.
    b. October.
    c. November.
    d. December.

6. Years ago when men on a ship would mutiny, the captain would punish the crew by *decimating* it; he would kill
    a. every seventh man.
    b. every eighth man.
    c. every ninth man.
    d. every tenth man.

7. Shakespeare was born in 1564. The year 1964 was the celebration of his
    a. centennial.
    b. bicentennial.
    c. tricentennial.
    d. quadricentennial.

8. A one-wheeled vehicle might be called a
    a. unicycle or a tricycle.
    b. unicycle or a quadricycle.
    c. monocycle or a unicycle.
    d. monocycle or a bicycle.

(continued)

© 1979 by Houghton Mifflin Company

9. Athletes who participate in the *decathlon* compete in
     a. six sports.
     b. eight sports.
     c. ten sports.
     d. twelve sports.

10. If something is *unique,* it is
     a. one of a kind.
     b. two of a kind.
     c. three of a kind.
     d. four of a kind.

11. My grandmother is seventy-one; my grandfather is ten years older, so he is
     a. a quinquagenarian.
     b. a sexagenarian.
     c. a septuagenarian.
     d. an octogenarian.

12. Which of the following is *octonary?*
     a. 16, 20, 24, 28
     b. 16, 22, 28, 34
     c. 16, 24, 32, 40
     d. 16, 26, 36, 46

13. Which of the following does not belong in this *monorhyme?*
     a. bad
     b. lad
     c. sad
     d. boy

14. The children were dichotomized into boys and girls, and then they were *trichotomized* into those who were
     a. 1-6 and 7-12 years old.
     b. 1-4, 5-8, and 9-12 years old.
     c. 1-3, 4-6, 7-9, and 10-12 years old.
     d. 1-2, 3-4, 5-6, 7-8, 9-10, and 11-12 years old.

© 1979 by Houghton Mifflin Company

PROPERTY OF
COMMUNICATION SKILLS CENTER
OHIO NORTHERN UNIVERSITY

Exercise 2

-Logy

The combining form *-logy* indicates "science" or "study of." For example, *mythology* is the study of myths. Also, the suffix *-ist* often indicates one who studies a particular subject—a *mythologist* studies mythology. Use this information to answer the following questions. The first problem has been solved for you:

1. *Anthropo-* indicates "man."

The study of the origin and the physical, social, and cultural development of humankind is called *anthropology* . An *anthropologist* studies this subject.

2. *Archaeo-* indicates "ancient times."

The study of objects that were left from life and culture in ancient times is called _____ . An _____ studies this subject.

3. *Audio-* indicates "hearing."

The study of hearing is called _____ . An _____ studies this subject.

4. *Bio-* indicates "life."

The study of the structure, functioning, growth, origin, evolution, and distribution of living things is called _____ . A _____ studies this subject.

5. *Chrono-* indicates "time."

The study of dates and the sequence of events in time is called _____ . A _____ studies this subject.

6. *Geo-* indicates "earth."

The study of the origin, history, and structure of the earth is

(*continued*)

called _____ . A _____ stud-

ies this subject.

7. *Gyneco-* (gyno-) indicates "woman."

The medical science and study of the diseases of women is called

_____ . A _____ studies this

science.

8. *Hydro-* indicates "water."

The study of the properties, distribution, and effects of water is

called _____ . A _____

studies this subject.

9. *Patho-* indicates "disease."

The scientific study of disease is called _____ .

A _____ studies this science.

10. *Psycho-* indicates "mind."

The scientific study of behavior and the processes of the mind is

called _____ . A _____

studies this subject.

11. *Seismo-* indicates "earthquake."

The scientific study of earthquakes is called _____ .

A _____ studies this subject.

12. *Theo-* indicates "gods" or "God."

The study of religious truth and the nature of God is called

_____ . A *theologian* (not a theologist) studies

this subject.

© 1979 by Houghton Mifflin Company

Exercise 3

-Phobia and -Mania

The combining form _-phobia_ indicates "a strong abnormal fear." Following are some phobias and the fears around which they center:

PHOBIA	FEAR
acrophobia	height
agoraphobia	open places
algophobia	pain
hemaphobia	blood
nyctophobia	darkness

Using the meanings of combining forms that were previously introduced in this chapter, you should be able to identify most of the objects of fear for the following phobias. If you do not know the meanings of _astra-, biblio-,_ or _pyro-,_ look them up in your dictionary.

PHOBIA	FEAR
1. anthrophobia	_____
2. astraphobia	_____
3. bibliophobia	_____
4. gynephobia	_____
5. hydrophobia	_____
6. pathophobia	_____
7. theophobia	_____
8. zoophobia	_____
9. pyrophobia	_____
10. monophobia	_____

The combining form _-mania_ indicates "a mental illness characterized by a craving for a particular thing." Following are some manias and the cravings around which they center:

(_continued_)

MANIA	CRAVING
acromania	heights
ailuromania	cats
cynomania	dogs
hypnomania	sleep
necromania	death

Using the meanings of combining forms that were previously introduced in this chapter, you should be able to identify most of the objects of craving for the following manias:

	MANIA	CRAVING
11.	hydromania	_____
12.	pyromania	_____
13.	theomania	_____
14.	monomania	_____
15.	zoomania	_____

© 1979 by Houghton Mifflin Company

Exercise 4

Bene-, -Cide, -Cracy, and -Archy

The combining form *bene-* indicates "good" or "well." It is contrasted with the prefix *mal-*, which means "wrong" or "bad."

1. If something is *bene*ficial for you, it is _____ for you.

2. If somebody you know has a tumor removed for fear of cancer, you would hope the tumor is
   a. benign.
   b. malignant.

3. It is *not* pleasant to be around people who do things that are
   a. benevolent.
   b. malicious.

4. Somebody who helps you achieve your goals is your
   a. benefactor.
   b. malefactor.

The combining form *-cide* indicates "to kill" or "killer."

5. An *insecticide* is used to kill _____.

6. *Infanticide* is the killing of a(n) _____.

7. *Femicide* must be the killing of a(n) _____.

8. A fraternity is a brotherhood of men; *fratricide* must be the killing of one's _____.

9. A sorority is a sisterhood of women; *sororicide* must be the killing of one's _____.

10. *Matricide* must be the killing of one's _____.

11. *Patricide* must be the killing of one's _____.

The combining forms *-cracy* and *-archy* both indicate "rule" or "government."

12. Who rules in a *mobocracy*? _____

13. Who rules in a *gynocracy*? _____

(*continued*)

14. Who rules in a *patriarchy?* _____

15. Who rules in a *matriarchy?* _____

16. Who heads a *theocracy?* _____

17. How many rule in a *monarchy?*_____

18. How many rule in a *polyarchy?*_____

© 1979 by Houghton Mifflin Company

Exercise 5   *Scientific and Technical Words*

The meanings of combining forms are especially important in most scientific and technical courses. *If you are studying a scientific or technical course at this time,* the following activities will help you understand how learning the meanings of combining forms can help you learn the meanings of complicated-looking words that are important in such courses.

1. Study the glossary or index of a scientific or technical textbook to find five sets of words that begin with the same spellings. There should be at least three words in each set you select. List the sets of words on a piece of paper. For example, if you are studying biology, this might be *one* of your five lists:

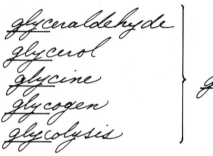

2. Use a desk dictionary or a dictionary in your library to determine if the spellings at the beginnings of the words indicate a combining form. For example, if you looked up *glyc-* this is what you might find:

> **glyco–, glyc–.** Indicates: **1.** Sugar; for example, **glycine.**
> **2.** Glycogen; for example, **glycogenesis.** [From Greek *glukus,*
> sweet. See d|ku- in Appendix.*]

When you find that spellings indicate combining forms, write their meanings next to the sets of words, just as "*glyc-* means 'sugar'" is written next to the set of words beginning with this spelling.

3. In your textbook, study the meanings of the words you listed together with the meanings of the combining forms to decide if learning the meanings of the combining forms will help you learn the meanings of the words in your lists.

© 1979 by Houghton Mifflin Company

SECTION 3

FINDING WORD MEANINGS IN REFERENCE SOURCES

Understanding how to analyze context (Chapters 2 through 4) and word structure (Chapters 5 through 9) to find the meanings of words greatly reduces the need to consult reference sources for the definitions of words. But, of course, there will be many times when you will not be able to determine the meanings of words from context and word structure.

Chapter 10 contains information and practice that should help you overcome any difficulties you have in finding the meanings of words in dictionaries. It also provides a means by which you can evaluate whether a dictionary is adequate for your needs.

Desk dictionaries, though, are not the only reference sources for information about words. *Chapter 11* explains how to use encyclopedias, specialized dictionaries, and other books to find more information about words than may be found in desk dictionaries and to find the meanings of words not defined in desk dictionaries.

Chapter 10   Dictionaries

When you cannot find the meanings of words by studying the contexts in which they appear or the word parts they contain, you will need to turn to a reference source—usually a dictionary. This chapter explains the kind of dictionary you should own and how to find the definitions you want when words have more than one meaning.

PAPERBACK DICTIONARIES VERSUS DESK DICTIONARIES

Paperback dictionaries are handy to carry, and they contain the meanings, pronunciations, and spellings of many common words. But college students who are interested in increasing their vocabularies will need to have a good desk dictionary as well as a paperback dictionary. The reason for this is that paperback dictionaries are short versions of longer, more complete dictionaries. For example, the 1,550 large pages of the desk edition of *The American Heritage Dictionary* were reduced to 820 small pages for the paperback edition. The paperback edition is an excellent value for its low price, but it cannot and does not contain everything in the college desk edition. In Figure 10.1 you will find an excerpt from the college desk edition of *The American Heritage Dictionary* and equivalent information from the paperback edition of this dictionary. Compare the information from these two books so you can understand why you should own a good desk dictionary.

You should own a paperback dictionary to carry with you to classes, but you should also own a good desk dictionary to use at home. There are several excellent desk dictionaries from which to

© 1979 by Houghton Mifflin Company

FIGURE 10.1 Paperback Dictionaries Versus Desk Dictionaries. Paperback dictionaries are convenient to use, but they do not contain all the information in a desk dictionary. Compare the information from *orifice* to *Orlon* in the desk edition of *The American Heritage Dictionary* (above in the figure) to the same information in the paperback edition of this dictionary (below).

or·i·fice (ôr'ə-fĭs, ŏr'-) *n.* A mouth or vent; an aperture of a cavity. [Old French, from Late Latin *ōrificium* : Latin *ōs* (stem *ōr-*), mouth (see **ōs-** in Appendix*) + *facere*, to make (see **dhē-¹** in Appendix*).]

or·i·flamme (ôr'ə-flăm', ŏr'-) *n.* Also **aur·i·flamme.** 1. The red or orange-red flag of the Abbey of St. Denis, France, used as a standard by the early kings of France. 2. Any inspiring standard or symbol. [Middle English *oriflamble*, from Old French *oriflambe*, from Medieval Latin *auriflamma* : Latin *aurum*, gold (see **aurum** in Appendix*) + *flamma*, FLAME.]

orig. original; originally.

o·ri·ga·mi (ôr'ĭ-gä'mē) *n.* 1. The art or process, originating in Japan, of folding paper into flower, bird, or other shapes. 2. A decorative object made in this way. Compare **kirigami.** [Japanese : *ori*, a folding + *-gami*, from *kami*, paper.]

Or·i·gen (ôr'ə-jən, ŏr'-). A.D. 185?–254? Christian teacher and theologian, born in Alexandria.

or·i·gin (ôr'ə-jĭn, ŏr'-) *n.* 1. That from which anything derives its existence; a source or cause. 2. Parentage; ancestry; derivation: *"We cannot escape our origins, however hard we try."* (James Baldwin). 3. A coming into being. 4. *Anatomy.* The point of attachment of a muscle. 5. *Mathematics.* The point of intersection of coordinate axes, as in the **Cartesian coordinate system** (*see*). [Middle English *origyne*, from Latin *orīgō* (stem *origin-*), from *orīrī*, to rise. See **er-¹** in Appendix.*]

Synonyms: origin, inception, source, root. These nouns relate to beginnings. *Origin*, applicable to persons as well as things, indicates the often remote place and time when something began. *Inception*, more specific, marks the actual start of an action or process. *Source*, also more specific, stresses the place from which something is derived or comes into being. It may also denote a person or printed work considered as a giver of information. *Root* usually refers to beginnings in the sense of fundamental cause or basic reason for something of consequence.

o·rig·i·nal (ə-rĭj'ə-nəl) *adj. Abbr.* **orig.** 1. Of or pertaining to the beginning of something; initial; first. 2. Fresh and unusual; not copied; new: *"some verses written by a famous painter which were original and not conventional"* (Emerson). 3. Able to produce new things; able to think of and present new ideas; creative; inventive. 4. Designating that from which a copy, reproduction, or translation is made. —See Synonyms at **new.** —*n. Abbr.* **orig.** 1. The primary form of anything from which varieties arise: *Later models retained many features of the original.* 2. An authentic work of art, literature, or the like, as distinguished from a copy or reproduction. 3. One that is the model for an artistic or literary work. 4. A peculiar, especially an eccentric person. [Middle English, from Old French, from Latin *originālis*, from *orīgō*, ORIGIN.]

o·rig·i·nal·i·ty (ə-rĭj'ə-năl'ə-tē) *n., pl.* **-ties.** 1. The quality of being original. 2. The capacity to act or think independently. 3. Something original.

o·rig·i·nal·ly (ə-rĭj'ən-əl-ē) *adv. Abbr.* **orig.** 1. With reference to origin. 2. At first. 3. In a highly distinctive manner.

original sin. *Theology.* 1. The tendency to evil inherent in human beings as a result of Adam's first act of disobedience. 2. *Roman Catholic Church.* The state of deprivation from grace resulting from Adam's sinful disobedience.

o·rig·i·nate (ə-rĭj'ə-nāt') *v.* **-nated, -nating, -nates.** —*tr.* To bring into being; create; invent. —*intr.* To come into being; start; spring. —**o·rig'i·na'tion** *n.* —**o·rig'i·na'tor** (-nā'tər) *n.* —**o·rig'i·na'tive** *adj.* —**o·rig'i·na'tive·ly** *adv.*

o·ri·na·sal (ôr'ĭ-nā'zəl, ŏr'-) *adj. Phonetics.* Pronounced with both nasal and oral passages open. —*n. Phonetics.* A sound, such as a French nasal vowel, pronounced in this way. [Latin *ōs* (stem *ōr-*), mouth (see **ōs-** in Appendix*) + NASAL.]

O·ri·no·co (ôr'ə-nō'kō, ŏr'-). A river rising in southeastern Venezuela and flowing 1,500 miles first west, then north, and then east to the Atlantic Ocean.

o·ri·ole (ôr'ē-ōl', ŏr'-) *n.* 1. Any of various Old World birds of the family Oriolidae, of which the males are characteristically bright-yellow and black. 2. Any of various New World birds of the family Icteridae, of which the males are black and orange or yellow. See **Baltimore oriole.** [French *oriol*, from Old French, from Medieval Latin *oriolus*, "golden (bird)," variant of Latin *aureolus*, diminutive of *aureus*, golden, from *aurum*, gold. See **aurum** in Appendix.*]

O·ri·on¹ (ō-rī'ən). *Greek Mythology.* A giant hunter, pursuer of the Pleiades and lover of Eos, killed by Artemis.

O·ri·on² (ō-rī'ən) *n.* A constellation in the celestial equator near Gemini and Taurus, containing the stars Betelgeuse and Rigel.

or·i·son (ôr'ə-sən, -zən, ŏr'-) *n.* A prayer. [Middle English, from Old French, from Latin *ōrātiō*, ORATION.]

O·ris·sa (ō-rĭs'ə, ō-rĭs'ə). A state in eastern India, 60,136 square miles in area, north of Tamil Nadu, on the Bay of Bengal. Population, 20,674,000. Capital, Bhubaneswar.

O·ri·ya (ō-rē'yə) *n.* An Indic language, spoken chiefly in Orissa, Republic of India.

O·ri·za·ba, Pi·co de (pē'kō thä ō'rē-sä'vä). *Aztec* **Ci·tlal·te·petl** (sē'tläl-tä'pĕt'l). An 18,700-foot volcanic peak, the highest elevation in Mexico, in central Veracruz State.

Or·khon (ôr'kŏn'). A river rising in central Mongolia and flowing 450 miles northeast to join the Selenga River.

Ork·ney Islands (ôrk'nē). Also **Ork·neys** (ôrk'nēz). *Abbr.* **Ork.** A cluster of islands, 376 square miles in area, off the northeastern coast of Scotland, of which they constitute a county. Population, 18,000. Capital, Kirkwall.

Or·lan·do (ōr-lăn'dō). A city and winter resort in central Florida. Population, 99,000.

Or·lan·do (ôr-län'dō), **Vittorio Emanuele.** 1860–1952. Prime Minister of Italy (1917–19).

Or·le·an·ist (ôr'lē-ə-nĭst) *n.* A supporter of the Orléans branch of the French royal family, descended from the Duke of Orléans, younger brother of Louis XIV.

Or·lé·ans (ôr-lā-äN'). A city in north-central France, on the Loire River south of Paris. Population, 84,000.

Or·lon (ôr'lŏn') *n.* A trademark for a synthetic acrylic fiber that is used alone or with other fibers in a variety of fabrics.

---

or·i·fice (ôr'ə-fĭs, ŏr'-) *n.* An opening; mouth; vent. [< LL *ōrificium.*]

orig. original; originally.

o·ri·ga·mi (ôr'ĭ-gä'mē) *n.* The Japanese art of folding paper into decorative shapes. [Jap.]

o·ri·gin (ôr'ə-jĭn, ŏr'-) *n.* 1. A source or cause of existence. 2. Ancestry; derivation. 3. A coming into being. 4. *Math.* The point of intersection of coordinate axes. [< L *orīrī*, to rise.]

o·rig·i·nal (ə-rĭj'ən-əl) *adj.* 1. Primary; first. 2. Fresh and novel. 3. Creative; inventive. —*n.* 1. The primary form from which copies are made or varieties arise. 2. An authentic work of art as distinguished from a copy. [< L *orīgō*, origin.] —**o·rig'i·nal'i·ty** (ə-rĭj'ə-năl'ə-tē) *n.* —**o·rig'i·nal·ly** *adv.*

o·rig·i·nate (ə-rĭj'ə-năt') *v.* **-nated, -nating.** To come or bring into being; begin. —**o·rig'i·na'tion** *n.* —**o·rig'i·na'tor** *n.*

O·ri·no·co (ôr'ə-nō'kō, ŏr'-). A river of NW South America.

o·ri·ole (ôr'ē-ōl', ŏr'-) *n.* A songbird with bright orange or yellow and black plumage. [< ML *oriolus*, "golden (bird)."]

O·ri·on (ō-rī'ən) *n.* A constellation on the celestial equator.

Or·lon (ôr'lŏn') *n.* A trademark for a synthetic fiber used in a variety of fabrics.

select. Following is a list of the ones most often recommended to college students:

> *The American Heritage Dictionary of the English Language, New College Edition*
> *Funk and Wagnalls Standard College Dictionary*
> *Random House Dictionary of the English Language: College Edition*
> *Webster's New World Dictionary of the American Language*
> *Webster's Seventh New Collegiate Dictionary*

These are all good dictionaries, but if you were to examine them closely you would find you prefer one or two of them to the others.

EXAMINING A DICTIONARY

If you find you do not use a dictionary very often, this may be because you do not own the one that is best for you. *When you own a dictionary that is the right one for you, you will find yourself using it more often, and, as a result, your vocabulary will grow.*

Opposite you will find a "Dictionary Checklist" you may use to rate a cloth-bound desk dictionary you own or are considering purchasing. If the dictionary you rate is a good one, the answers to all the questions on the checklist will be "yes." However, the answers to some questions are more important than others. If the definitions in a dictionary are not easy for you to understand, the dictionary will not be useful to you even if the answers to all the other questions are "yes."

© 1979 by Houghton Mifflin Company

Dictionary Checklist

Use this checklist to determine if a dictionary you own or are considering purchasing contains all the features you need in a dictionary. Write the title of the dictionary you are evaluating:

Title: _____

YES   NO

_____ _____ 1. The **publication date** of the dictionary is no more than eight years old.

_____ _____ 2. The **definitions** for words are easy to understand.

_____ _____ 3. **Biographical information** is given (look up the name of a famous person in history).

_____ _____ 4. **Geographical information** is given (look up the name of a famous city, country, mountain, or body of water).

_____ _____ 5. **Foreign phrases** are defined (look up *bête noire*).

_____ _____ 6. **Homographs** are labeled with raised numbers (look up *banker* to see if you find "banker¹," "banker²," and "banker³ ").

_____ _____ 7. Some derivatives are listed as **run-ons** (look up *dependable* to see if you find *dependability, dependableness,* and *dependably* listed at the end of the definition of *dependable*).

_____ _____ 8. **Prefixes** are defined (look up *pseudo-*).

_____ _____ 9. **Suffixes** are defined (look up *-ist*).

_____ _____ 10. **Combining forms** are defined (look up *helio-*).

_____ _____ 11. **Abbreviations** are defined (look up *P.S.*).

_____ _____ 12. The dictionary has good **pictures, illustrations,** and **maps.**

_____ _____ 13. Some definitions have **subject labels** (look up *depression* to see if some definitions are labeled "Meteorology," "Economics," "Astronomy," or "Psychology").

_____ _____ 14. Some definitions have **usage labels** (look up *bug* to see if a definition is labeled "Informal"—or "Colloquial"—and if a definition is labeled "Slang").

_____ _____ 15. Meanings of **synonyms** are discussed (look up *old* to see if following its definitions there is a discussion of the differences among such synonyms as *ancient, antique,* and *archaic*).

FINDING THE RIGHT DEFINITION FOR A WORD

One of the biggest problems in using a dictionary is that since many words have more than one meaning, it is often difficult to find exactly the meaning that is wanted. For example, this dictionary entry lists many meanings for the word *compound:*

com·pound[1] (kŏm-pound′, kəm-) *v.* **-pounded, -pounding, -pounds.** —*tr.* **1.** To combine; mix. **2.** To produce or create by combining two or more ingredients or parts. **3.** *Pharmacology.* To mix (drugs) according to prescription. **4.** To settle (a debt, for example) by agreeing on an amount less than the claim; adjust. **5.** To compute (interest) on the principal and accrued interest. **6.** *Law.* To agree, for payment or other consideration, not to prosecute: *compound a felony.* **7.** To add to; increase. —*intr.* **1.** To come to terms; agree. **2.** To settle or compromise with a creditor. —See Synonyms at **mix.** —*adj.* (kŏm′pound, kŏm-pound′). Consisting of two or more substances, ingredients, elements, or parts. —*n.* (kŏm′pound). *Abbr.* **comp., cpd. 1.** A combination of two or more elements or parts. **2.** A combination of words or word elements regarded as a unit according to various linguistic analyses, as: **a.** A graphemic unit containing two or more free forms, or one or more free forms with one or more bound forms, with or without hyphenation. **b.** A word containing two or more elements that have perceptible lexical meaning. **c.** An intonational pattern exhibiting a primary stress and a terminal juncture. **d.** A sequence of words not connected by a functional element in surface structure but functioning as a grammatical kernel in deep structure. **3.** *Chemistry.* A pure, macroscopically homogeneous substance consisting of atoms or ions of two or more different elements in definite proportions, and usually having properties unlike those of its constituent elements. —See Synonyms at **mixture.** [Middle English *compounen,* from Old French *compon(d)re,* from Latin *compōnere,* to put together : *com-,* together + *pōnere,* to put (see **apo-** in Appendix*).] —**com·pound′a·ble** *adj.* —**com·pound′er** *n.*

Some people do not use dictionaries often because they become frustrated when they cannot locate the definitions they want in listings such as this one for *compound.* If this has ever been a source of difficulty for you, the problems for this chapter will help you become more confident that you will find the definitions you want when you look for them in a dictionary.

PRACTICE PROBLEMS

The practice problems for this chapter require you to find the correct definitions for words when they have more than one meaning. Following is a sample problem, its solution, and an explanation of how to solve the problems:

© 1979 by Houghton Mifflin Company

coach (kōch) *n.* **1.** A large closed carriage with four wheels. **2.** A closed automobile, usually with two doors. **3.** A motor-bus. **4.** A railroad passenger car. **5.** A low-priced class of passenger accommodations on a train or airplane. **6.** A person who trains athletes or athletic teams. **7.** A private tutor employed to prepare a student for an examination. —*v.* **coached, coaching, coaches.** —*tr.* **1.** To teach or train; tutor. **2.** To transport by coach. —*intr.* **1.** To act as a coach. **2.** To ride in a coach. [French *coche,* from German *Kutsche,* from Hungarian *kocsi,* after *Kocs,* a town in Györ, Hungary, where such carriages originated.] —**coach′er** *n.*

_6_ 1. The **coach** gave us a pep talk before the game.

_1_ 2. A company in Los Angeles rents **coaches** to people who make Western movies and television shows.

_5_ 3. It is cheaper to fly **coach** than to go first class.

Solve the problems by writing the number of the definition that is specified by the context in which the word appears. Also:

1. Do not use a definition as the answer to more than one question.

2. If there is more than one sequence of numbers for definitions, select all your answers from the first sequence of numbers. (There are three sequences of numbers for definitions of *coach,* but the answers were all selected from the first sequence of numbers.)

© 1979 by Houghton Mifflin Company

Exercise 1

Definitions for Words

The directions for solving these problems are given under "Practice Problems."

pan·o·ram·a (păn'ə-răm'ə, -rä'mə) *n.* **1.** An unlimited view of all visible objects over a wide area. **2.** A comprehensive picture of a chain of events or a specific subject: *a panorama of ancient history.* **3.** A picture or series of pictures representing a continuous scene, exhibited a part at a time by being unrolled and passed before the spectator. [PAN- + Greek *horāma*, sight, from *horān*, to see (see **wer-**⁴ in Appendix*).] —**pan'o·ram'ic** *adj.* —**pan'o·ram'i·cal·ly** *adv.*

_____ **1.** As we took off from the Seattle-Tacoma Airport, we had a **panorama** of the Olympic Mountains to our right and the Cascade Mountains to our left.

_____ **2.** The exhibition provides a **panorama** of French art from 1850 to 1900.

_____ **3.** In motion pictures, a **panorama** is filmed by turning the camera so that a wide angle of the surroundings is taken in.

po·tent (pōt'nt) *adj.* **1.** Possessing inner or physical strength; powerful. **2.** Capable of commanding attention; able to convince: *potent arguments.* **3.** Having great control or authority: *"The police were potent only so long as they were feared."* (Thomas Burke). **4.** Capable of causing strong physiological or chemical effects, as medicines or alcoholic beverages. **5.** Able to perform sexually. Said of a male. [Middle English (Scottish), from Latin *potēns*, present participle of Old Latin *potēre* (unattested) (superseded by *posse*), to be able, have power. See **poti-** in Appendix*.] —**po'tent·ly** *adv.* —**po'tent·ness** *n.*

_____ **4.** Franklin Roosevelt was a **potent** leader during the depression of the 1930s and the war of the 1940s.

_____ **5.** Regular aspirin is too **potent** for small children.

_____ **6.** If the wife is fertile and the husband is **potent**, they should be able to have children.

(continued)

com·pose (kəm-pōz′) v. -posed, -posing, -poses. —tr. 1. To make up the constituent parts of; constitute or form. See Usage note at comprise. 2. To make or create by putting together parts or elements. 3. To create or produce (a literary or musical piece). 4. To make (one's mind or body) calm or tranquil; to quiet. 5. To settle (arguments); reconcile. 6. To arrange aesthetically or artistically. 7. *Printing.* To arrange or set (type or matter to be printed). —intr. 1. To create literary or musical pieces. 2. *Printing.* To set type. [Middle English, from Old French *composer* : *com-*, together, from Latin + *poser*, to place, from Latin *pausāre*, to cease, repose, hence to place, from *pausa*, a pause, from Greek *pausis*, from *pauein*, to stop (see **pauein** in Appendix*).]

_____ 7. Waldorf salad is **composed** of apples, nuts, celery, and mayonnaise.

_____ 8. When you are overly excited, you may **compose** yourself by taking a few deep breaths.

_____ 9. Bach and Beethoven **composed** some of the best-known classical music.

rem·nant (rĕm′nənt) n. 1. Something left over; a remainder. 2. A leftover piece of fabric, as one remaining after the rest of the bolt has been sold. 3. A surviving trace or vestige, as of a former condition. 4. *Often plural.* A small, remaining group of people. —See Synonyms at remainder. —adj. Remaining; leftover. [Middle English *remenant*, from Old French, present participle of *remanoir, remaindre*, to REMAIN.]

_____ 10. The bump at the bottom of your spine is a **remnant** of a tail!

_____ 11. All the **remnants** I liked were not large enough to make a shirt.

_____ 12. The tribe of thirty are the **remnants** of a thriving Stone Age culture.

© 1979 by Houghton Mifflin Company

Exercise 2   *Definitions for Words*

The directions for solving these problems are given just before the first exercise for this chapter.

brass (brăs, bräs) *n.* **1.** An alloy of copper and zinc with other metals in varying lesser amounts. **2.** Ornaments, objects, or utensils made of brass. **3.** *Plural. Music.* Wind instruments, such as the French horn and trombone, made of brass. **4.** A memorial plaque or tablet made of brass. **5.** *Machinery.* A bushing sleeve or similar lining for a bearing, made from a copper alloy. **6.** *Informal.* Blatant self-assurance; effrontery; nerve. **7.** *Slang.* High-ranking military officers or other high officials. **8.** *British Slang.* Money. [Middle English *bras,* Old English *bræs.* See **ferrum** in Appendix.*] —**brass** *adj.*

_____ **1.** The soldier wanted to go home on leave, but the **brass** wouldn't let him.

_____ **2.** He has the **brass** to tell anybody exactly what he thinks.

_____ **3.** Many belt buckles are made of **brass.**

fa·tigue (fə-tēg′) *n.* **1.** Physical or mental weariness or exhaustion resulting from exertion. **2.** Tiring effort or activity; labor. **3.** *Physiology.* The decreased capacity or complete inability of an organism, organ, or part to function normally because of excessive stimulation or prolonged exertion. **4.** Weakness in metal, wood, or other material resulting from prolonged stress. **5.** *Military.* Manual or menial labor, such as barracks cleaning assigned to soldiers: *a weekend on fatigue.* Also called "fatigue duty." **6.** *Plural. Military.* Clothing designated or permitted for work and field duty. —*v.* **fatigued, -tiguing, -tigues.** —*tr.* **1.** To tire out; exhaust. **2.** To weaken by prolonged stress. —*intr.* To be or become exhausted or tired out. [French, from Old French, from *fatiguer,* to fatigue, from Latin *fatīgāre†.*]

_____ **4.** The bridge collapsed from the **fatigue** of two hundred years of use.

_____ **5. Fatigues** are worn during all field training at Army training camps.

_____ **6.** Our best pitcher couldn't play ball for two weeks because his pitching arm needed to recover from **fatigue.**

(*continued*)

dis·ci·pline (dĭs′ə-plĭn) *n.* **1.** Training that is expected to produce a specified character or pattern of behavior, especially that which is expected to produce moral or mental improvement. **2.** Controlled behavior resulting from such training. **3.** A systematic method to obtain obedience: *a military discipline.* **4.** A state of order based upon submission to rules and authority. **5.** Punishment intended to correct or train. **6.** A set of rules or methods, as those regulating the practice of a church or monastic order. **7.** A branch of knowledge or of teaching. —*tr.v.* **disciplined, -plining, -plines. 1.** To train by instruction and control; teach to obey rules or accept authority. **2.** To punish or penalize. —See Synonyms at **teach, punish.** [Middle English, from Old French, from Latin *disciplīna, discipulīna,* instruction, knowledge, from *discipulus,* pupil, DISCIPLE.] —**dis′ci·plin′er** *n.*

_____ **7.** Few people have the **discipline** necessary to do well as a student while holding a full-time job.

_____ **8.** In some high schools special deans **discipline** uncooperative students.

_____ **9.** Professor Simpson is an expert in three **disciplines**—literature, art, and philosophy.

in·duce (ĭn-dōōs′, -dyōōs′) *tr.v.* **-duced, -ducing, -duces. 1.** To lead or move by influence or persuasion; to prevail upon: *finally induced him to give up smoking.* **2.** To stimulate the occurrence of; cause: *induce childbirth.* **3.** To infer by inductive reasoning. **4.** *Physics.* To produce (an electric current or magnetic effect) by induction. —See Synonyms at **persuade.** [Middle English *inducen,* from Latin *indūcere : in-,* in + *dūcere,* to lead (see **deuk-** in Appendix*).] —**in·duc′er** *n.* —**in·duc′i·ble** *adj.*

_____ **10.** I get it! You're saying that if the angles of each of these different kinds of triangles add up to 180 degrees, then I'm to **induce** that the angles of *all* triangles add up to 180 degrees.

_____ **11.** Since all their children had moved to California, they were **induced** to move there also.

_____ **12.** In some cases a solution of warm, salty water will **induce** vomiting.

© 1979 by Houghton Mifflin Company

Exercise 3   _Definitions for Words_

The directions for solving these problems are given just before the first exercise for this chapter.

> **con·ven·tion** (kən-vĕn′shən) _n. Abbr._ **conv. 1.** A formal assembly or meeting of members, representatives, or delegates of a group, such as a political party or fraternal society. **2.** The body of persons attending such an assembly. **3.** An agreement or compact; especially, an international agreement dealing with a specific subject, as the treatment of war prisoners. **4.** General agreement on or acceptance of certain practices or attitudes. **5.** A practice or procedure widely observed in a group, especially to facilitate social intercourse; custom. **6.** A widely used and accepted device or technique, as in drama, literature, or painting: _the theatrical convention of the "aside."_ [Middle English _convencioun,_ from Old French _convention,_ from Latin _conventiō,_ assembly, agreement, from _convenire,_ to come together, CONVENE.]

_____ **1.** The question "How do you do?" is a **convention** that gives us something to say when we meet strangers.

_____ **2.** A **convention** of English teachers was held in New Orleans last year.

_____ **3.** The close-up is a **convention** of movie making that gives movies an intimacy that is difficult to achieve in live theater.

> **cat·a·ract** (kăt′ə-răkt′) _n._ **1.** A very large waterfall. **2.** A great downpour. **3.** _Pathology._ Opacity of the lens or capsule of the eye, causing partial or total blindness. [Middle English _cataracte,_ floodgate, from Old French, portcullis, cataract (of the eye), from Latin _catarractēs,_ waterfall, portcullis, from Greek _katar(rh)aktēs,_ "a down-swooping," from _katarassein,_ to dash down : _kata-,_ down + _rassein,_ to strike (see **wrāgh-²** in Appendix*).]

_____ **4.** I suggest you stay indoors; there is no way to dress properly for this **cataract**.

_____ **5.** In Niagara you will find one of the world's most famous **cataracts**.

_____ **6.** A contact lens is often prescribed for people who have a **cataract** removed.

(_continued_)

sti·fle¹ (stī′fəl) *v.* **-fled, -fling, -fles.** —*tr.* **1.** To kill by preventing respiration; smother or suffocate. **2.** To interrupt or cut off (the voice or breath). **3.** To keep or hold back; suppress; repress: *stifle one's views.* —*intr.* **1.** To die of suffocation. **2.** To feel smothered or suffocated by or as if by close confinement in a stuffy room. — See Synonyms at **suppress.** [Middle English *stufflen,* probably formed as a frequentative from Old French *estouffer,* to choke, smother, from Vulgar Latin *extuffāre* (unattested), perhaps alteration (influenced by unattested *extūfāre,* to bathe in hot vapor, STEW) of *stuppāre* (unattested), to stop up with tow, from Latin *stuppa,* tow, from Greek *stuppē.* See **stewe-** in Appendix.*] —**sti′fler** *n.* —**sti′fling·ly** *adv.*

_____ 7. The judge had the defendants gagged to **stifle** their protests.

_____ 8. He tried to preserve harmony in the family by **stifling** his dislike for the thoughtless remarks of some of his relatives.

_____ 9. Toward the end of the play, Othello kills his wife by **stifling** her with a pillow.

mar·tyr (mär′tər) *n.* **1.** One who chooses to suffer death rather than renounce religious principles. **2.** One who sacrifices something very important to him in order to further a belief, cause, or principle. **3.** A person who endures great suffering. **4.** A person who makes a great show of suffering in order to arouse sympathy: *"For to feel oneself a martyr, as everybody knows, is a pleasurable thing."* (Erskine Childers). —*tr.v.* **martyred, -tyring, -tyrs.** **1.** To make a martyr of (a person). **2.** To inflict great pain upon; torment: *"martyr'd by the gout"* (Pope). [Middle English *martir,* Old English *martyr,* from Late Latin *martyr,* from Greek *martus†* (stem *martur-*), witness, witness (of Christ).]

_____ 10. He is such a **martyr** about going to the grocery store that I'd rather go myself than listen to him complain.

_____ 11. Many early Christians became **martyrs** when they were burned at the stake, crucified, or thrown to the lions rather than give up their beliefs.

_____ 12. Martin Luther King, Jr., was a **martyr** for civil rights.

© 1979 by Houghton Mifflin Company

Exercise 4   _Definitions for Words_

The directions for solving these problems are given just before the first exercise for this chapter.

> **in·te·grate** (ĭn′tə-grāt′) _v._ **-grated, -grating, -grates.** —_tr._ **1.** To make into a whole by bringing all parts together; unify. **2.** To join with something else; to unite. **3.** To open to people of all races or ethnic groups without restriction; desegregate. **4.** _Mathematics._ **a.** To calculate the integral of. **b.** To perform integration upon. **5.** To bring about the integration of (personality traits). —_intr._ To become integrated or undergo integration. [Latin _integrāre_, to make complete, from _integer_, whole. See **integer.**] —**in′te·gra′tive** _adj._

_____ **1.** The songs were beautiful, the play was good, and the dancing was superb, but somehow they were not **integrated** into an effective musical comedy.

_____ **2.** If the construction crew is not **integrated,** federal money cannot be used to construct the highway.

_____ **3.** She is an interesting history professor because in her lectures she **integrates** history with literature, music, art, and philosophy.

> **e·merge** (ĭ-mûrj′) _intr.v._ **emerged, emerging, emerges. 1.** To rise up or come forth from or as if from immersion; come into sight. **2.** To become evident or obvious. **3.** To issue, as from obscurity or an unfortunate condition: _"We have seen how the Church emerged from this welter of barbarism."_ (G.G. Coulton). **4.** To crop up; come into existence. [Latin _ēmergere_ : _ex-_, out of + _mergere_, to dip, immerse (see **mezg-**¹ in Appendix*).]

_____ **4.** Every now and then a great leader **emerges** from the faceless crowd.

_____ **5.** The sun will **emerge** from behind the mountain at approximately six o'clock tomorrow morning.

_____ **6.** Your talent for parenthood cannot **emerge** until you actually have children to care for.

(_continued_)

em·i·nent (ĕm'ə-nənt) *adj.* **1.** Towering above others; projecting; prominent: *the Empire State Building, eminent among the skyscrapers.* **2. a.** Outstanding in performance or character; distinguished: *an eminent historian.* **b.** Of high rank or station. **3.** Possessed or shown to a remarkable degree; noteworthy: *a man esteemed for his eminent achievements.* [Middle English, from Old French, from Latin *ēminēns,* present participle of *ēminēre,* to stand out : *ex-,* out + *-minēre,* to stand, project (see **men-²** in Appendix*).] —**em'i·nent·ly** *adv.*

_____ 7. The Eiffel Tower is **eminent** in the Paris skyline.

_____ 8. Her achievements in national and international relations made Eleanor Roosevelt an **eminent** citizen of the United States and the world.

_____ 9. John Kenneth Galbraith is an **eminent** twentieth-century economist.

sham (shăm) *n.* **1.** Something false or empty purporting to be genuine; a spurious imitation. **2.** The quality of deceitfulness; empty pretense. **3.** A person who assumes a false character; a pretender or impostor: *"He a man! Hell! He was a hollow sham!"* (Conrad). **4.** A decorative cover made to simulate an article of household linen and used over or in place of it: *a pillow sham.* —*adj.* Not genuine; fake, pretended, or counterfeit. —*v.* **shammed, shamming, shams.** —*tr.* **1.** To put on the false appearance of; feign. **2.** *Obsolete.* To deceive. —*intr.* To assume a false appearance or character; dissemble. [Possibly variant of SHAME.] —**sham'mer** *n.*

_____ 10. She's a master of **sham,** an expert at using her smile to cover the lies she cannot resist telling.

_____ 11. He is a **sham**—he uses big words, but he doesn't know what they mean.

_____ 12. The menu said "strawberries and whipped cream," but this white stuff is a **sham** for real cream.

© 1979 by Houghton Mifflin Company

Chapter 11   Other Reference Sources

There will be many times when you will want more information about words than is given in a good desk dictionary. This will be especially true when words name persons, places, or things. A good desk dictionary will, for example, give some information about *Fidel Castro, Savannah,* and *trichinosis,* but, as the following dictionary entries suggest, it may not give all the information you want about words such as these:

Cas·tro (kăs′trō; *Spanish* käs′trō), **Fidel.** In full, Fidel Castro Ruz. Born 1927. Cuban revolutionary; premier (since 1959).

Sa·van·nah (sə-văn′ə). A seaport and the oldest city of Georgia, at the mouth of the Savannah River. Population, 114,000.

trich·i·no·sis (trĭk′ə-nō′sĭs) *n.* A disease caused by eating inadequately cooked pork containing trichinae, and characterized by intestinal disorders, fever, muscular swelling, pain, and insomnia. [New Latin : TRICHIN(A) + -OSIS.]

Such dictionary information is helpful; however, there is much more to be known about Fidel Castro, the information about Savannah is inadequate if you are planning to visit or move to that city, and the facts about trichinosis are insufficient if you fear you are suffering from this disease.

There are three basic sources to which you can turn when you want more information about words than is given in a dictionary: (1) encyclopedias, (2) specialized dictionaries, and (3) other books. This chapter explains how to find information about words in these sources.

ENCYCLOPEDIAS

If you want more information about a word that names a well-known person, place, or thing, an encyclopedia is likely to give you a great deal of help. For example, if you looked up the meaning of *syphilis* in a dictionary, the definition might not be complete enough for your purposes:

> **syph·i·lis** (sĭf′ə-lĭs) *n.* A chronic infectious venereal disease caused by a spirochete, *Treponema pallidum,* transmitted by direct contact, usually in sexual intercourse, and progressing through three stages respectively characterized by local formation of chancres, ulcerous skin eruptions, and systemic infection leading to general paresis. [New Latin, after *Syphilis,* title character of a Latin poem (1530) by Girolamo Fracastoro, Veronese physician and poet and the supposed first victim of the disease.]

Compare this dictionary entry for *syphilis* to this information, which appears in the one-volume *New Columbia Encyclopedia:*

Cause — **syphilis** (sĭf′ə-lĭs), contagious disease, the most serious of the VENEREAL DISEASES, caused by a spirochete, *Treponema pallidum* (described by F. R. Schaudinn and Eric Hoffmann in 1905). Syphilis first appeared in Spain among sailors who had returned from the New World in 1493. It was carried into Italy by the armies of Charles VIII of France and spread throughout Europe, being known variously as Neapolitan disease and French pox. — History

How transmitted — The most prevalent mode of transmission is by sexual contact; infection by other means is possible, but its occurrence depends upon an open wound or lesion to permit invasion of the organisms. Transmission may also occur through infected blood or plasma and from an infected mother to her fetus.

The development of syphilis occurs in three stages. The primary stage is the appearance of a chancre at the site of infection about three or four weeks after contact, with enlargement of the regional lymph nodes. There are no other symptoms. The secondary stage usually begins with a generalized eruption of the skin and mucous membranes; there may be inflammatory involvement of the eyes, bones, liver, heart, or central nervous system. Tests of the blood serum give proof of infection; many states require such tests before issuing marriage licenses. The tertiary stage is characterized by skin lesions that tend to be chronic and destructive, by tumors in the subcutaneous tissues and in the internal organs, severe damage to the heart and aorta, and progressive central nervous system involvement including locomotor ataxia, degeneration of the optic nerves with possible blindness, and insanity. — Stages

Cure — Until the advent of penicillin during the 1940s, specific and protracted treatment for syphilis was with arsenic, mercury, and bismuth. Present-day therapy is with penicillin for all stages and types of syphilis. The early stage of the disease, and in most cases the secondary stage also, can be cured with penicillin. Even central nervous system syphilis may be cured by penicillin if damage to the

© 1979 by Houghton Mifflin Company

nerve tissue has not begun. The incidence of syphilis and other venereal diseases in the United States has been rising, especially among teenagers and homosexuals, causing renewed concern among public health officials.* | Frequency

As you can see, the encyclopedia information about syphilis is much more complete than the definition given in a dictionary. Some of the following encyclopedias devote two or more pages to even fuller discussions of syphilis and thousands of other topics:

Encyclopaedia Britannica
Encyclopedia Americana
Chambers's Encyclopaedia
Collier's Encyclopedia
World Book Encyclopedia

Of these encyclopedias, the *World Book* and *Collier's* are written to be easiest to understand. It is wise to study encyclopedias whenever you want concise information on any subject.

SPECIALIZED DICTIONARIES Libraries have specialized dictionaries for subjects ranging from sports to medicine and from fashion to technology. These dictionaries not only often give more information about words than is given in desk dictionaries, *specialized dictionaries also often give the meanings of words that are not defined in desk dictionaries.*

You may find the specialized dictionaries you need by seeking the help of a librarian or by consulting a card catalog. Specialized dictionaries are listed on subject cards that have titles such as the following:

MEDICINE–DICTIONARIES
BIOGRAPHY–DICTIONARIES
SPORTS–DICTIONARIES
MUSIC–DICTIONARIES
MATHEMATICS–DICTIONARIES

*Reprinted from the *New Columbia Encyclopedia*, New York: Columbia University Press, 1975.

Figure 11.1 shows the subject card headed "United States—Biography—Dictionary" that was used to find *Webster's American Biographies*. This reference book contains detailed information of the type shown in Figure 11.2. A librarian can help you find this and other kinds of information in your library.

FIGURE 11.1 A Subject Card That Was Helpful in Finding Information About Famous Americans. See Figure 11.2 for an example of the type of information contained in *Webster's American Biographies*.

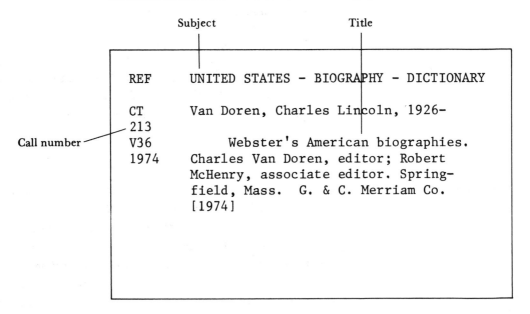

© 1979 by Houghton Mifflin Company

FIGURE 11.2 A Passage from *Webster's American Biographies*. This passage about Helen Keller illustrates one type of information that can be found in specialized dictionaries. (By permission. From Webster's American Biographies © 1975 by G. & C. Merriam Co., Publishers of the Merriam-Webster Dictionaries.)

Keller, Helen Adams (1880–1968), author and lecturer. Born on June 27, 1880, near Tuscumbia, Alabama, Helen Keller was afflicted at the age of 19 months with an illness that left her blind, deaf, and mute. She was examined by Alexander Graham Bell at about the age of six; as a result he sent to her a twenty-year-old teacher, Anne Mansfield Sullivan, from the Perkins Institution, which Bell's son-in-law directed. Miss Sullivan (later Mrs. John A. Macy), a remarkable teacher, remained with Helen from March 2, 1887, until her death in 1936. Within months Helen had learned to feel objects and associate them with words spelled out by finger signals on her palm, to read sentences by feeling raised words on cardboard, and to make her own sentences by arranging words in a frame. During 1888–1890 she spent winters in Boston at the Perkins Institution learning Braille. Then she began a slow process of learning to speak—feeling the position of the tongue and lips, making sounds, and imitating the lip and tongue motions—at Boston's Horace Mann School for the Deaf. She also learned to lip-read by placing her fingers on the lips and throat of the speaker while the words were simultaneously spelled out for her. At fourteen she enrolled in the Wright-Humason School for the Deaf in New York City, and at sixteen entered the Cambridge School for Young Ladies in Massachusetts. She won admission to Radcliffe College, entering in 1900, and graduated cum laude in 1904. Having developed skills never approached by any person so handicapped, she began to write of blindness, a subject then taboo in women's magazines because of the relationship of many cases to venereal disease. The pioneering editor Edward W. Bok accepted her articles for the *Ladies' Home Journal*, and other major magazines—*The Century, McClure's,* and the *Atlantic Monthly*—followed suit. She wrote of her life in several books, including *The Story of My Life,* 1902; *Optimism,* 1903; *The World I Live In,* 1908; *Song of the Stone Wall,* 1910; *Out of the Dark,* 1913; *My Religion,* 1927; *Midstream,* 1929; *Peace at Eventide,* 1932; *Helen Keller's Journal,* 1938; *Let Us Have Faith,* 1940; and *The Open Door,* 1957. In 1913 she began lecturing, primarily on behalf of the American Foundation for the Blind, for which she established a $2-million endowment fund, and her lecture tours took her around the world. Her efforts to improve treatment of the deaf and the blind were influential in removing the handicapped from asylums. She also prompted the organization of commissions for the blind in 30 states by 1937. Awarded the Presidential Medal of Freedom in 1963, she died in Westport, Connecticut, on June 1, 1968, universally acknowledged as one of the great women of the world.

BOOKS

Books, of course, also give detailed information about words. Your textbooks and many books you find in a library have glossaries and indexes to help you find information about the words discussed in them.

Glossaries. A *glossary* is a list of definitions of words that are important for understanding a book. Glossaries are usually found at the ends of books, but sometimes there is a short glossary at the end of each chapter in a book. Figure 11.3 shows part of a glossary from a book on psychology. Some of the definitions in the glossary are similar to definitions in dictionaries. Compare the following dictionary definition of *reality principle* to the definition given in Figure 11.3:

reality principle. *Psychoanalysis.* Awareness of and adjustment to environmental demands in a manner that assures ultimate satisfaction of instinctual needs.

Often, though, glossaries contain definitions that cannot be found in desk dictionaries. Several of the words defined in Figure 11.3 are not defined in desk dictionaries (for example, *rational therapy, reactive schizophrenia,* and *reality testing*).

FIGURE 11.3 **Part of a Glossary from a Book on the Subject of Psychology. (From BASIC PSYCHOLOGY, 3rd edition, by Norman L. Munn, L. Dodge Fernald, and Peter S. Fernald. Copyright © 1972 by Houghton Mifflin Company. Used by permission.)**

rating The degree to which some trait is said to be present, as judged from observation or from the subject's report.

rational therapy Therapeutic procedures based on the premise that lack of information or illogical thought patterns are basic causes of the patient's difficulties. Furthermore, it is assumed that the individual can be assisted in overcoming his problems by a direct, prescriptive, advice-giving approach by the therapist.

rationalization Finding "good" but false reasons for actions. Making what is irrational appear rational. Excusing one's actions on irrational grounds.

reaction formation Excluding a desire from awareness by repressing it and assuming the opposite attitude.

reaction time Speed of reaction to a stimulus.

reactive schizophrenia A schizophrenic condition the onset of which involves an acute and sudden reaction to severe environmental pressure.

readiness The time, resulting largely from maturational factors, when the organism is first capable of responding correctly to a task.

reality principle The principle that the demands of the id usually must be adapted to actualities in the physical and social environment. Awareness of the conditions of the environment.

reality testing A term used by Freud to refer to the exploratory or probing behavior by which the individual learns about his environment. Basic to development of the ego.

reasoning Solving some problem implicitly, using symbols to represent objects or situations. Thinking one's way through a problem rather than engaging in overt trial and error.

recall Revival of past experience; remembering a past event by only a few cues.

reception learning Learning in which the subject is given the material in approximately final form, as in a lecture situation. The subject's task is to commit the material to memory.

receptor A specialized end organ which receives stimulation. The receptors of the eyes, for example, are the rods and cones.

receptor-effector system The system which connects receptors and effectors, including, of course, the central nervous system.

recessive gene See *dominance.*

recitation In learning, trying at intervals to recall and recite what one is memorizing, as opposed to merely reading it repeatedly.

recognition Perceiving something as having been experienced before, as being familiar.

© 1979 by Houghton Mifflin Company

Indexes. If a book has a good *index,* the meanings of words explained in the book may be found easily even if it has no glossary. Figure 11.4 shows part of an index from a book on the subject of business. This index may be used to find information about *population growth, insurance premiums, price lines,* and so on.

When books contain a glossary and an index, consult both when trying to find the meanings of words. If a word is defined in a glossary and elsewhere in a book, *the definition found by using the index is likely to be more complete.*

FIGURE 11.4 Part of an Index from a Book on the Subject of Business. Explanations found by using an index are usually more complete than those found in a glossary. (From MODERN BUSINESS, 2nd edition, by S. B. Rosenblatt, R. L. Bonnington, and B. E. Needles, Jr. Copyright © 1977 by Houghton Mifflin Company. Used by permission.)

© 1979 by Houghton Mifflin Company

Exercise   In a dictionary, select a word that names a person, place, or thing. The word you choose should be well known and discussed in dictionaries *and* encyclopedias. For example, *Sigmund Freud, San Francisco,* and *dreams* are all well-known words that are discussed in these two types of reference sources.

1. Write the word you chose:

_____

2. Select a desk dictionary in which to find information about this word. Write the title of the dictionary you chose:

_____

3. Write the information the desk dictionary gives about the word:

_____

_____

_____

_____

4. In a library, find an encyclopedia that gives information about this word. Write the title of the encyclopedia:

_____

5. How many pages of information does the encyclopedia give about the word? _____

6. Check if, in your opinion, the information in the encyclopedia is

       _____ very informative.

       _____ informative.

       _____ not very informative.

7. In a library, find a specialized dictionary that gives information about this word. Write the title of the specialized dictionary:

_____

(continued)

8. Check if, in your opinion, the information in the specialized dictionary is

            _____ much more informative than the information in the desk dictionary.

            _____ a little more informative than the information in the desk dictionary.

            _____ not as informative as the information in the desk dictionary.

9. In a library, find a book that gives information about this word. Write the title of the book and its author's name:

_____

_____

10. How many pages of information does this book give about the word? _____

11. Check if, in your opinion, the information in the book is

            _____ very informative.

            _____ informative.

            _____ not very informative.

12. Number the following reference sources 1, 2, 3, and 4, in the order of their usefulness for finding information about the word you researched:

            _____ desk dictionary

            _____ encyclopedia

            _____ specialized dictionary

            _____ book

© 1979 by Houghton Mifflin Company

PART II

INCREASING YOUR WRITING AND SPEAKING VOCABULARY

Part I of this book was devoted to helping you increase the number of words you know when you read or listen by teaching you to use context, word structure, and reference sources to find the meanings of words. The reasons for this emphasis are:

1. Words must be in your reading and listening vocabulary *before* they can become part of your writing and speaking vocabulary.

2. If you have a large reading and listening vocabulary, you have the potential for having a large writing and speaking vocabulary. However, if you have a small reading and listening vocabulary, there is no way you can have a large writing and speaking vocabulary.

The last five chapters in this book explain the things you can do to move words from your listening and reading vocabulary into your writing and speaking vocabulary. *Chapter 12* explains methods you can use to systematically learn words you would like to use when you write and speak. You are not likely to use a word when you speak if you do not know how to pronounce it. *Chapter 13* teaches you how to use a dictionary to find pronunciations for words. Also, you are likely to be uncomfortable using a word when you write if you are not certain how to spell it. *Chapter 14* explains how to use a dictionary to find the correct spellings of words. Often, knowing the origins of words can help you learn and remember them. *Chapter 15* explains some interesting ways words came into English and how you can find this type of information about words. A final way to increase your writing and speaking vocabulary is to actively seek "new" words to express your thoughts. In *Chapter 16* you will learn how to use a dictionary to find interesting words to add to your writing and speaking vocabulary.

© 1979 by Houghton Mifflin Company

Chapter 12   Learning New Words

This chapter explains how you can take words from your reading and listening vocabulary and make them part of your writing and speaking vocabulary. The things you can learn from this chapter are important because *your writing and speaking vocabulary is enlarged only when you decide you will use words in writing and speaking that you have never used for these purposes before.* Unless you make the decision to use new words when you write and speak, your writing and speaking vocabulary will never be any larger than it is today!

LEARNING NEW WORDS IN YOUR COLLEGE COURSES

An extremely practical way for you to increase your writing and speaking vocabulary is to make a conscious effort to learn the words you need to learn in the college courses you are studying. You will need to learn many new words in every course you take, and if you learn the words you *need* to learn, you will find many of them will be words you will *want* to use in your general vocabulary.

For example, in a psychology course you may need to learn such words as *anxiety, extraversion, manipulation, perception,* and *somatic.* In an English course you may need to learn such words as *infer, ambiguous, paradox, allusion,* and *exposition.* Learning words such as these not only will help you do better in psychology and English courses but also will enrich your general vocabulary.

FIGURE 12.1 Examples of Words That You Might Need to Learn for Courses You Are Taking, but That You Can Also Use in Your General Vocabulary

WORDS FROM AN ENGLISH COURSE

denotation	subjective	colloquial
connotation	ambiguity	narration
generalization	euphemism	exposition
theory	redundancy	description
inductive	paradox	idiom
deductive	stereotype	jargon
fallacy	irony	cliché
assumption	sarcasm	paraphrase
infer	wit	plagiarism
imply	analogy	syllabication
objective	allusion	pejorative

WORDS FROM A PSYCHOLOGY COURSE

assertive	taboos	apathy
defensive	anxiety	biofeedback
hostile	cognition	ethics
extraversion	empathy	inhibition
introvert	hierarchy	manipulation
heredity	ingenuity	phobic
latent	maladaptive	psychotherapy
perception	scapegoat	self-esteem
placebos	somatic	statistics
rationalization	validity	suppression
rituals	ambivalence	vicarious

In Figure 12.1 there are examples of other words of this type that you might need to learn in an English or psychology course. Similar lists could be made for any college course, including scientific and technical courses.

In each course you take, you will find many words that you must learn, but there are also other types of words that you may

© 1979 by Houghton Mifflin Company

FIGURE 12.2 Examples of Words That You Probably Will Not *Need* to Learn for Courses You Take in College but May *Want* to Learn for Your Own Satisfaction and Vocabulary Growth

presumptuous	advocate	agnostic	amenable
protocol	autonomy	avenge	benevolence
recalcitrant	bucolic	capricious	catastrophe
sardonic	charlatan	chauvinism	clandestine
sophisticated	complacent	continual	continuous
succinct	culpable	cynical	decimate
tirade	definitive	demolition	deprecate
prognosis	dichotomy	dour	duress
quintessence	elicit	elucidate	elude
resilient	epicure	epitome	erotic
secular	feasible	flaccid	flaunt
sporadic	flout	fortuitous	gargantuan
supersede	genocide	gratuitous	gregarious
tortuous	herculean	hypothesis	illicit
protagonist	implication	incorrigible	inculcate
quixotic	insidious	intrepid	irrevocable
revenge	judicious	juxtaposition	longevity
segregate	luxuriant	malefactor	masochism
subjugate	maudlin	meander	mentor
sycophant	mercurial	mimicry	minutiae
preposterous	narcissism	neophyte	omnipotent
posthumous	omniscient	ostracism	panacea
potpourri	pediatrician	peripatetic	philanderer

wish to add to your vocabulary. These are words you may feel belong in the vocabulary of a well-educated person. You may be intrigued by such words as *vicarious* (which means "to experience through others"), *garrulous* (which means "talkative"), or *ubiquitous* (which means "seeming to be everywhere at the same time"). Figure 12.2 lists other words of this type. You may very well wish to expand your vocabulary to include such colorful and expressive words—and you can!

ORGANIZING WORDS FOR LEARNING

The many new words that you will want to learn in college will need to be well organized so they can be learned easily. You may use 3-inch by 5-inch index cards or a notebook to organize the words you want to learn. Figure 12.3 shows a 3-inch by 5-inch

FIGURE 12.3 An Example of How to Prepare 3-Inch by 5-Inch Index Cards to Learn the Meanings of Words in Courses You Are Taking. The word to be learned is written boldly on the blank side of the card, and then the card is flipped over (upside-down) to write the definition on the back.

FRONT

Plagiarism

BACK

© 1979 by Houghton Mifflin Company

index card for learning the meaning of a word in an English course, and Figure 12.4 shows a page from a notebook set up for learning the meanings of words in a psychology course. Either index cards or notebooks offer a good method for organizing words you wish to learn.

**THREE STEPS
FOR LEARNING WORDS**

You can learn the meanings of words by (1) reciting them, (2) using the words in conversation, and (3) using them in writing.

Recitation. *Recitation* is the act of saying information to yourself so that you will be able to recall it when you want to. You can recite the meanings of words that you have written on 3-inch by 5-inch index cards or in notebooks by reading a word whose meaning you want to learn and then saying its meaning aloud without looking at the definition you have written. For example, in reciting the word on the card in Figure 12.3, you would read "plagiarism," and then, without looking at the back of the card, you would try to say the definition to yourself: "The act of passing off somebody else's ideas or words as your own. For example, copying what somebody else wrote and offering it as your own."

When reciting from notebooks, cover the meanings of words by folding the notebook page. Turn to Figure 12.4 and fold the page forward to the dashed line. Folding the page in this way ensures that the meanings of words in notebooks are hidden during recitation.

Using New Words in Conversation. If you use words in conversation, they become part of your speaking vocabulary. Three practical ways to give yourself an opportunity to use new words in speech are to study with a friend, to participate in class discussions, and to explain things you learn to friends or relatives.

Find a classmate in each course you take, and arrange times when you get together for study. You can test each other on the things you are learning, or perhaps you will find that even informal discussions about what you are studying in your courses will give you an opportunity to use the new words you are learning.

Taking part in classroom discussions will also give you an excellent opportunity to use and learn new words. If you find it difficult to take part in discussions, carefully prepare questions you want answered in your courses. You might find it helpful to write out your questions and to memorize them before you ask them in classes. This is a good way to ease yourself into the habit of participating in discussions.

Finally, you probably have a friend or relative who is interested to know what you are learning in college. If so, you will help yourself learn new words by explaining their meanings to such people and by using these words in your conversations with them as often as possible.

Using New Words in Writing. You use new words in writing when you write papers for your courses and take essay tests. When you write papers for your courses, use the new words you have learned; and when you take essay tests, prepare for them by writing practice answers to questions you expect will be on the tests.

PRACTICE PROBLEMS

This chapter explained how you can begin today to expand your vocabulary by learning the words you need to learn in the courses you are taking and any other words you want to learn for any purpose you may have. The following exercises will help you understand the suggestions by putting them to use.

Exercise 1

Use the example in Figure 12.3 to make *at least* thirty (30) 3-inch by 5-inch index cards to learn words in a course you are taking. Use the methods described in this chapter to study the words in preparation for a test in the course.

Exercise 2

Use the example in Figure 12.4 to make a notebook of *at least* fifty (50) words to learn in a course you are taking. Use the methods described in this chapter to study the words in preparation for a test in the course.

© 1979 by Houghton Mifflin Company

FIGURE 12.4 An Example of How to Organize Notebook Pages for Learning Words in Courses You Are Taking. Notice that the definitions are set apart from the words so the meanings may be easily covered during recitation. To cover the meanings, simply fold the page forward to the dashed line.

extravert	A person who is more concerned with socializing than with attending to what is going on in his or her mind (Jung).
introvert	A person who, when faced with a problem, tends to withdraw into himself or herself and to avoid others (Jung).
empiricism	The view that behavior is learned as a result of experience.
conscience	A personal standard of right and wrong that an individual uses to judge what he or she does.
dissonance	The difference between what people think they believe and what they do (Festinger).

FIGURE 12.5   A Card for Learning a Word. A complete card for learning a word contains not only the word and its definition, but also (1) its pronunciation, when you are not sure how the word is pronounced, (2) its etymology, when the etymology is helpful for learning the word, and (3) synonyms, if the word has any.

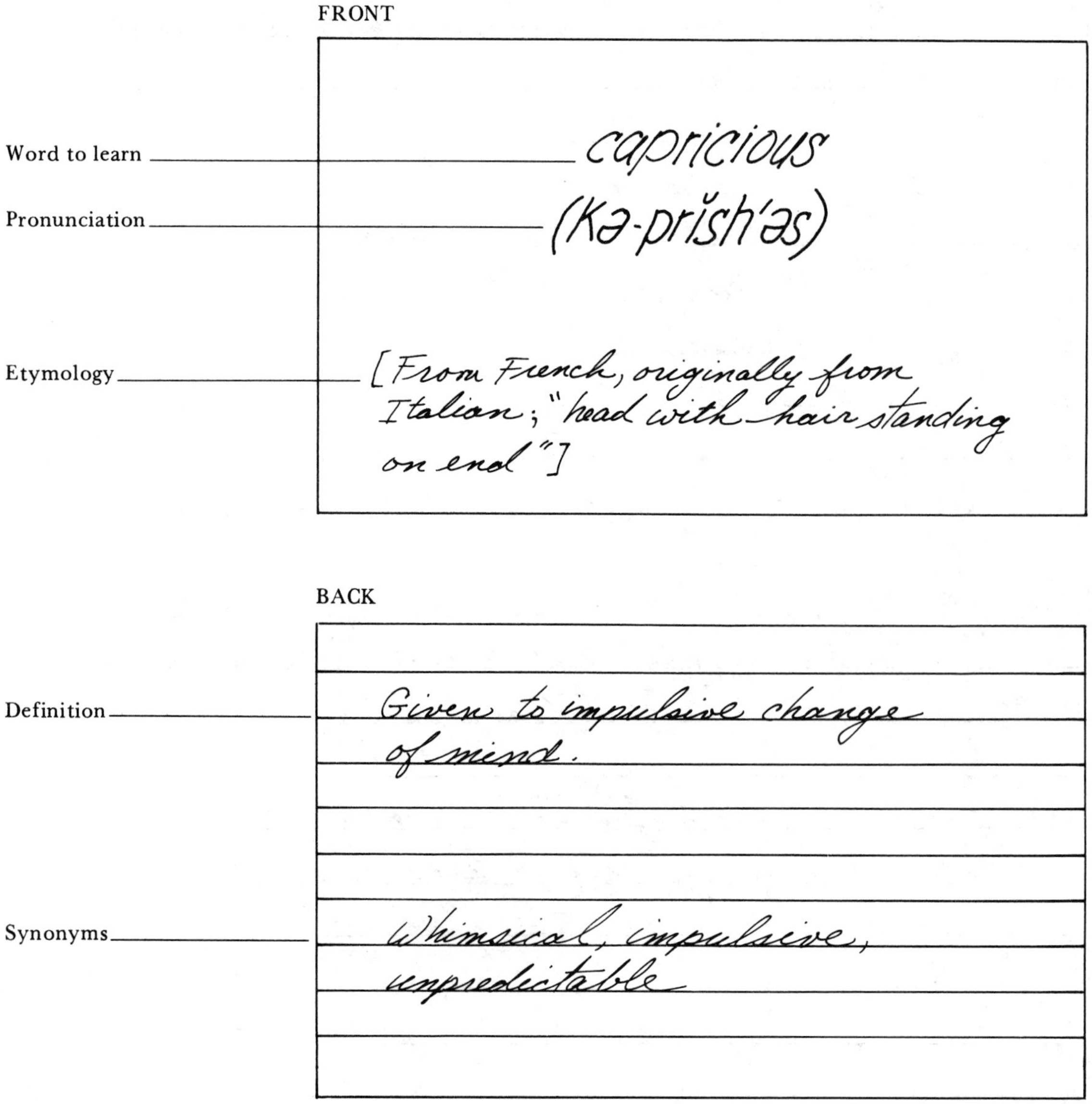

FRONT

Word to learn ——————— capricious

Pronunciation ——————— (Kə-prĭsh′əs)

Etymology ——————— [From French, originally from Italian; "head with hair standing on end "]

BACK

Definition ——————— Given to impulsive change of mind.

Synonyms ——————— Whimsical, impulsive, unpredictable

© 1979 by Houghton Mifflin Company

Exercise 3

After you have studied Chapters 13, 15, and 16, make a set of 3-inch by 5-inch index cards to learn the meanings of the words listed in Figure 12.2. Use your dictionary to find information about pronunciations, etymologies, and synonyms, so you can make cards as shown in Figure 12.5. Then use the methods described in this chapter to prepare for a test on the meanings of the words.

Chapter 13   Pronunciation

Do you ever avoid using a word simply because you are not certain how to pronounce it? Most of us are embarrassed when we are told we pronounced a word incorrectly, and, as a result, we often tend to avoid using words when we are uncertain of their pronunciations. If you avoid using a word because you are not certain how to pronounce it, the word will never become a part of your speaking vocabulary. It is for this reason that understanding how to find the pronunciations of words is an important part of vocabulary growth.

For the most part we learn how to pronounce words by listening to others pronounce them. You will learn to pronounce many new words while you are in college because you will hear them pronounced during lectures and class discussions. But you do not need to rely solely on the pronunciations of others in order to know how words are pronounced. Dictionaries provide information that you can use to determine the pronunciations of words even if you have never heard them pronounced before.

PRONUNCIATION SPELLINGS   In dictionaries, words are respelled using special markings so their pronunciations may be learned. In the following respelling you can see that the *m* at the beginning of *mnemonic* is not pronounced:

Pronunciation
spelling

> **mne·mon·ic** (nĭ-mŏn′ĭk) *adj.* Relating to, assisting, or designed to assist the memory. —*n.* A device, such as a formula or rhyme, used as an aid in remembering. [Medieval Latin *mnēmonicus,* from Greek *mnēmonikos,* from *mnēmōn,* mindful. See **men-**¹ in Appendix.*] —**mne·mon′i·cal·ly** *adv.*

© 1979 by Houghton Mifflin Company

138

Pronunciation spellings, such as this one for *mnemonic,* are interpreted using a pronunciation key that appears at the bottoms of dictionary pages. A *pronunciation key* explains the sounds that letters represent. Following is an example of a pronunciation key:

ă pat/ā pay/âr care/ä father/b bib/ch church/d deed/ĕ pet/ē be/f fife/g gag/h hat/hw which/ĭ pit/ī pie/îr pier/j judge/k kick/l lid, needle/m mum/n no, sudden/ng thing/ŏ pot/ō toe/ô paw, for/oi noise/ou out/o͝o took/o͞o boot/p pop/r roar/s sauce/sh ship, dish/ t tight/th thin, path/*th* this, bathe/ŭ cut/ûr urge/v valve/w with/y yes/z zebra, size/zh vision/ə about, item, edible, gallop, circus/ à *Fr.* ami/œ *Fr.* feu, *Ger.* schön/ü *Fr.* tu, *Ger.* über/KH *Ger.* ich, *Scot.* loch/N *Fr.* bon. ***Follows main vocabulary.** †**Of obscure origin.**

If this pronunciation key were used to interpret the pronunciation of *mnemonic* (nĭ-mŏn′ĭk), the interpretation would be as follows:

n	as in *n*o
ĭ	as in p*i*t
m	as in *m*um
ŏ	as in p*o*t
n	as in *n*o
ĭ	as in p*i*t
k	as in *k*ick

The exercises in this chapter will help you learn how to use a pronunciation key such as the one shown above to determine the pronunciations of words. *Since not all dictionaries use the same pronunciation key, the exercises emphasize the most frequent sounds in words and sounds that are represented similarly in many modern dictionaries.*

LONG AND SHORT VOWEL SOUNDS

Say the names of the letters *a, e, i, o,* and *u* aloud. The sounds you heard when you said "*a, e, i, o, u*" are the *long sounds* of vowels. They are usually shown this way in pronunciation respellings: ā, ē, ī, ō, and yo͞o. Following are the pronunciation spellings of some words that have long vowel sounds:

hate	(hāt)
beat	(bēt)
kite	(kīt)
goat	(gōt)
tube	(tyo͞ob)

Say these words aloud: *hat, bet, kit, got, tub*. The vowel sounds you heard in the middle of these words are the *short sounds* of vowels. They are usually shown this way in pronunciation spellings: ă, ĕ, ĭ, ŏ, and ŭ. Following are the pronunciation spellings of some words that have short vowel sounds:

hat	(hăt)
bet	(bĕt)
kit	(kĭt)
got	(gŏt)
tub	(tŭb)

It is important that you understand the differences among short and long vowel sounds before you learn about other vowel sounds. Use this information to solve the problems in Exercise 1.

Exercise 1   *Long and Short Vowel Sounds*

Write the English spellings for the following pronunciation spellings. The first two have been done for you.

1. (flăp) *flap*
2. (kīt) *kite*
3. (sĕd) _____
4. (hŏp) _____
5. (plān) _____
6. (bĕl) _____
7. (wīn) _____
8. (mŏp) _____
9. (păst) _____
10. (mēt) _____
11. (rĭd) _____
12. (slōp) _____
13. (fāt) _____
14. (twĭnz) _____
15. (wēd) _____
16. (nōt) _____
17. (frām) _____
18. (spĕk) _____
19. (slīm) _____
20. (bōn) _____
21. (rān) _____
22. (stēm) _____

(continued)

© 1979 by Houghton Mifflin Company

23. (spīt) _____   32. (blŏk) _____

24. (glŏb) _____   33. (plăn) _____

25. (băk) _____   34. (pĕk) _____

26. (bēt) _____   35. (strĭp) _____

27. (dĭm) _____   36. (hōp) _____

28. (rōb) _____   37. (hāt) _____

29. (măn) _____   38. (sĕl) _____

30. (mēn) _____   39. (spīn) _____

31. (shīn) _____   40. (tōst) _____

THE SOUNDS OF o͞o, yo͞o, AND o͝o

The sounds of o͞o, yo͞o, and o͝o are very easy to confuse when reading pronunciation spellings. Exercise 2 will help you understand the differences among them.

1. The sound of o͞o is the one you hear in *blue* and *broom:*

     blue   (blo͞o)
     broom   (bro͞om)

2. The sound of yo͞o is the one you hear in *few:*

     few   (fyo͞o)

Notice that this sound is the same as o͞o, except it is pronounced with a *y* before it: yo͞o. This is the *long sound* of *u*—the sound you hear when you pronounce the letter *u* when saying the alphabet.

3. The sound of o͝o is the one you hear in *cook* and *put:*

     cook   (ko͝ok)
     put   (po͝ot)

Learn the differences among these three vowel sounds by solving the problems in Exercise 2.

Exercise 2   *The Sounds of $\overline{oo}$, y$\overline{oo}$, and $\breve{oo}$*

Write the English spellings for the following pronunciation spellings. The first three have been done for you.

1. (k$\overline{oo}$l)   *cool*
2. (b$\breve{oo}$k)   *book*
3. (my$\overline{oo}$l)   *mule*
4. (f$\breve{oo}$t) _____
5. (f$\overline{oo}$l) _____
6. (h$\breve{oo}$d) _____
7. (h$\overline{oo}$p) _____
8. (m$\overline{oo}$n) _____
9. (fy$\overline{oo}$m) _____
10. (r$\overline{oo}$m) _____
11. (sh$\breve{oo}$k) _____
12. (w$\breve{oo}$d) _____
13. (py$\overline{oo}$r) _____
14. (k$\breve{oo}$k) _____
15. (s$\overline{oo}$n) _____
16. (g$\breve{oo}$d) _____
17. (ky$\overline{oo}$t) _____
18. (z$\overline{oo}$m) _____
19. (l$\breve{oo}$k) _____
20. (f$\overline{oo}$d) _____

21. (t$\breve{oo}$k) _____
22. (ky$\overline{oo}$b) _____
23. (w$\breve{oo}$l) _____
24. (g$\overline{oo}$f) _____
25. (m$\overline{oo}$d) _____
26. (hy$\overline{oo}$j) _____
27. (fy$\overline{oo}$z) _____
28. (h$\breve{oo}$k) _____
29. (p$\overline{oo}$l) _____
30. (t$\overline{oo}$l) _____
31. (n$\breve{oo}$k) _____
32. (my$\overline{oo}$t) _____
33. (st$\breve{oo}$d) _____
34. (z$\overline{oo}$) _____
35. (sh$\overline{oo}$t) _____
36. (br$\breve{oo}$k) _____
37. (y$\overline{oo}$z) _____
38. (sp$\overline{oo}$n) _____
39. (kr$\breve{oo}$k) _____
40. (br$\overline{oo}$m) _____

© 1979 by Houghton Mifflin Company

THE SOUNDS OF oi, ou,
AND ô

There are three additional vowel sounds that are represented similarly in the pronunciation keys of most modern dictionaries.

1. The sound of *oi* as in *soil* and *toy:*

    soil   (soil)
    toy   (toi)

2. The sound of *ou* as in *bow-wow* and *bound:*

    bow-wow   (bou′wou′)
    bound   (bound)

3. The sound of ô, as in *law:*

    law   (lô)

Also you should have noticed in doing Exercises 1 and 2 that some
consonant letters are not used in pronunciation spellings. They are
the letters *c, q,* and *x.* The letter *c* is usually pronounced *k* or *s:*

    *c*at   (*k*ăt)
    *c*ent   (*s*ĕnt)

The letter *q* is usually pronounced *kw:*

    *q*uack   (*kw*ăk)

And the letter *x* is usually pronounced *ks* or *z:*

    ta*x*   (tă*ks*)
    *X*erox   (*z*îr′ŏks)

You will need to keep these things in mind as you solve the problems for Exercise 3.

Exercise 3   *The Sounds of oi, ou, and ô*

Write the English spellings for the following pronunciation spellings. The first three have been done for you.

1. (rānj)   *range*
2. (kwĭt)   *quit*
3. (wăks)   *wax*
4. (ēz)   _____
5. (fīt)   _____
6. (gōst)   _____
7. (dăns)   _____
8. (jĕm)   _____
9. (hĭz)   _____
10. (nŏk)   _____
11. (thŭm)   _____
12. (shŏŏd)   _____
13. (drô)   _____
14. (doun)   _____
15. (joi)   _____
16. (krīm)   _____
17. (fōn)   _____
18. (kŏf)   _____
19. (prōōn)   _____
20. (kloud)   _____

21. (chois)   _____
22. (fās)   _____
23. (mīt)   _____
24. (kwēn)   _____
25. (fôls)   _____
26. (boi)   _____
27. (rās)   _____
28. (nīs)   _____
29. (fĭks)   _____
30. (kŏŏd)   _____
31. (rô)   _____
32. (kloun)   _____
33. (kôz)   _____
34. (dīs)   _____
35. (koin)   _____
36. (sô)   _____
37. (kroud)   _____
38. (dŭz)   _____
39. (pā)   _____
40. (broun)   _____

© 1979 by Houghton Mifflin Company

THE SCHWA (ə)

One of the most useful vowel sounds in pronunciation spellings is represented by a symbol that does not appear in our alphabet. This symbol is the *schwa* (ə), which looks like an upside-down *e*. The sound of schwa is sometimes represented by the spelling *uh:*

*a*lone   (uh-lōn′) or (ə-lōn′)

The sound of schwa may be spelled by *a, e, i, o,* or *u:*

*a*lone	(ə-lōn′)
it*e*m	(ī′təm)
eas*i*ly	(ē′zə-lē)
lem*o*n	(lĕm′ən)
*u*pon	(ə-pŏn′)

The accent marks (′) in the pronunciation spellings show what part of the words is emphasized. For example, the first part of *item* is accented, while the second part of *alone* is accented:

i′tem
a-lone′

Say these words aloud and you will hear the accent on the first part of *item* and on the second part of *alone.*

Use all the things you have learned to solve the problems in Exercises 4 and 5.

Exercise 4

The Schwa

Write the English spellings for the following pronunciation spellings. The first one has been done for you.

1. (byo͞o′tə-fəl)   *beautiful*

2. (ăk′shən)   _____

3. (ə-dĭsh′ən)   _____

4. (ăd-vĕn′chər)   _____

5. (ôl-rĕd′ē)   _____

(continued)

6. (kŭm′pə-nē)   _____

7. (ôl′wāz)   _____

8. (kən-dĭsh′ən)   _____

9. (fĭg′yər)   _____

10. (kən-tĭn′yo͞o)   _____

11. (hyo͞o′mən)   _____

12. (hŭz′bənd)   _____

13. (ĭn-krēs′)   _____

14. (năsh′ən-əl)   _____

15. (pĭk′chər)   _____

16. (pŏs′ə-bəl)   _____

17. (prĕz′ə-dənt)   _____

18. (kwĕs′chən)   _____

19. (kwī′ĭt)   _____

20. (kăp′tən)   _____

Exercise 5

The Schwa

Write the English spellings for the following pronunciation spellings. The first one has been done for you.

1. (sĕn′chə-rē)   *century*_____

2. (kăr′ĭk-tər)   _____

3. (shə-kô′gō)   _____

4. (kŏl′ĭj)   _____

5. (dô′tər)   _____

6. (dĭ-stroi′)   _____

© 1979 by Houghton Mifflin Company

(continued)

7. (dĭ-rĕk′shən) _____

8. (dĭs-kŭv′ər) _____

9. (ĭng′glənd) _____

10. (ĕk-spĭr′ē-əns) _____

11. (jĕn′ər-əl) _____

12. (jĕnt′l-mən) _____

13. (ĭn′dē-ən) _____

14. (ī′lənd) _____

15. (ĭsh′o͞o) _____

16. (mĕzh′ər) _____

17. (mĭl′yən) _____

18. (năch′ər-əl) _____

19. (nā′bər) _____

20. (ô′fĭ-sər) _____

OTHER SOUNDS IN WORDS

This chapter gave you practice with the most frequently occurring vowel and consonant sounds in English words so you will feel comfortable using the pronunciation key at the bottoms of pages in your dictionary.

When you study the pronunciation key in your dictionary, you will find speech sounds that have not been discussed here; however, you will also discover that what you practiced in this chapter will be very helpful in learning to use the pronunciation key in your dictionary. Start soon to develop your skills at translating pronunciation spellings and you will always be able to find correct pronunciations for words so you can add them to your speaking vocabulary.

Chapter 14   Spelling

When you write, do you ever avoid using a word because you are not certain of its spelling? If you avoid using a word because you are not certain how to spell it, the word will never become a part of your writing vocabulary. It is for this reason that understanding how to find the spellings of words is an important part of vocabulary growth.

How do you rate your spelling?

> Perfect?
> Very good?
> Better than most people's?
> Not very good?
> Poor?

If you rate your spelling less than perfect, the information in this chapter will help you start spelling better. One characteristic of good spellers is that they know when to use a dictionary to find the correct spellings of words; *this chapter will help you understand when you should consult a dictionary to assure yourself that you have spelled a word correctly.*

Instruction is focused on six major spelling problems that can be easily solved by consulting a good desk dictionary. They are:

1. Should I drop the final *e* before adding a suffix? (Should I spell *valueable* or *valuable?*)
2. Should I change *y* to *i* before adding a suffix? (Should I spell *monkies* or *monkeys?*)
3. Should I double the final consonant before adding a suffix? (Should I spell *alloted* or *allotted?*)

© 1979 by Houghton Mifflin Company

4. Should I spell *ie* or *ei?* (Should I spell *receive* or *recieve?*)

5. Should I spell a consonant sound with one consonant or two consonants? (Should I spell *occasion, ocasion, ocassion,* or *occassion?*)

6. Should I spell the sound of schwa (ə) with *a, e, i, o,* or *u?* (Should I spell maint*e*nance, maint*a*nance, or maint*i*nance?)

The information and practice in this chapter will help you learn how to find the answers to questions such as these, so you may avoid six spelling problems that account for a high proportion of misspelled words.

BASE WORDS ENDING WITH *e*

When base words end with a final silent *e*, the *e* is sometimes dropped before suffixes are added. The rule is:

> *When words end in* e, *the* e *is usually dropped before suffixes that begin with a vowel but* not *before suffixes that begin with a consonant.*

The following dictionary entry shows how the rule applies to *revolve.* Notice that when *-ed, -ing,* and *-able* are added to *revolve,* the *e* is dropped to spell *revolved, revolving,* and *revolvable.*

Adding *-ed* and *-ing*

re·volve (rĭ-vŏlv′) *v.* **-volved, -volving, -volves.** —*intr.* **1.** To orbit a central point. **2.** To turn on an axis; rotate. **3.** To recur in cycles or at periodic intervals. **4.** To be held in the mind and considered in turn. —*tr.* **1.** To cause to revolve. **2.** To think over; ponder or reflect on. —See Synonyms at **turn.** [Middle English *revolven,* from Latin *revolvere,* to roll back : *re-,* back + *volvere,* to roll (see **wel-³** in Appendix*).] —**re·volv′a·ble** *adj.*

Adding *-able*

If you are uncertain of how to add a suffix to a base word that ends in final silent *e,* you will find the answer in a good desk dictionary.

Exercise 1

Base Words Ending with e

The rule for adding endings to words that end in final silent *e* applies to all but four of the following words. Use the rule given above and your dictionary to help you find the correct spellings of the words. The first two have been done for you.

1. pleasure + -able   *pleasurable*
2. lone + -ly   *lonely*
3. advertise + -ment   _____
4. admire + -ing   _____
5. judge + -ment   _____
6. white + -ness   _____
7. value + able   _____
8. acre + -age   _____
9. immediate + -ly   _____
10. like + -able   _____
11. argue + -ment   _____
12. mature + -ity   _____
13. confuse + -ion   _____
14. enforce + -ment   _____
15. acknowledge + -ment _____

BASE WORDS ENDING WITH *y*

When base words end with *y*, the *y* is sometimes changed to *i* before suffixes are added. The rule is:

> *When words end in* y, *the* y *is usually changed to* i *before a suffix if there is a consonant in front of the* y *but not if there is a vowel in front of the* y.

The following dictionary entry shows how the rule applies to *convey*. Notice that when *-ed, -ing, -s,* and *-able* are added to *convey*, the *y* is not changed to *i* because there is a vowel in front of the *y*.

© 1979 by Houghton Mifflin Company

Adding -ed,
-ing, and -s

con·vey (kən-vā′) *tr.v.* **-veyed, -veying, -veys.** **1.** To take or carry from one place to another; to transport. **2.** To serve as a medium of transmission for; to conduct; transmit. **3.** To communicate or make known; impart: *"a look intended to convey sympathetic comprehension"* (Saki). **4.** *Law.* To transfer ownership of or title to. **5.** *Obsolete.* To steal. [Middle English *conveien,* from Old French *conveier,* from Medieval Latin *conviāre,* to go with, escort : Latin *com-,* with + *via,* way (see **wei-²** in Appendix*).] **—con·vey′a·ble** *adj.*

Adding *-able*

If you are uncertain how to add a suffix to a word that ends in *y,* you will find the answer in a good desk dictionary.

Exercise 2

Base Words Ending with y

The rule for adding endings to words that end in *y* applies to all but three of the following words. Use the rule given above and your dictionary to help you find the correct spellings of the words. The first two have been done for you.

1. happy + -ness　　*happiness*
2. play + -ful　　*playful*
3. lonely + -ness　　_____
4. mystery + -ous　　_____
5. pay + -able　　_____
6. sly + -ness　　_____
7. pretty + -ness　　_____
8. annoy + -ance　　_____
9. study + -ing　　_____
10. merry + -est　　_____
11. attorney + -s　　_____
12. destroy + -er　　_____

(*continued*)

13. enjoy + -ment _____

14. shy + -ly _____

15. silly + -ness _____

**DOUBLING
FINAL CONSONANTS**

Sometimes the consonant at the end of a base word is doubled before a suffix is added. The rule is:

When words end in one *consonant, the consonant is usually doubled before endings that begin with a vowel if* (1) *the word is accented at the end and* (2) *there is only* one *vowel in front of the final consonant.*

The following dictionary entry shows how the rule applies to *remit.* Notice that *remit* ends with one consonant, that there is only one vowel in front of the consonant, and that *remit* is accented at the end (re-mit′). When suffixes that begin with vowels are added to *remit,* the final consonant is doubled: remi*tt*ed, remi*tt*ing, remi*tt*able, and remi*tt*or.

Adding *-ed*
and *-ing*

re·mit (rǐ-mǐt′) *v.* **-mitted, -mitting, -mits.** —*tr.* **1.** To send (money); transmit. **2. a.** To cancel (a penalty or punishment). **b.** To pardon; forgive. **3.** To restore to an original condition; put back. **4.** *Law.* To refer (a case) back to a lower court for further consideration. **5.** To relax; slacken. **6.** To defer; postpone. —*intr.* **1.** To transmit money. **2.** To diminish; abate. [Middle English *remitten,* from Latin *remittere,* to send back, release : *re-,* back + *mittere,* to send (see **smeit-** in Appendix*).] —**re·mit′ta·ble** *adj.* —**re·mit′tor** (rǐ-mǐt′ər) *n.*

Adding *-able*
and *-or*

When you are not certain if you should double a final consonant, you can find the correct spelling in a dictionary.

Exercise 3

Doubling Final Consonants

The rule for doubling final consonants applies to *all* the words in this exercise. However, since this rule is difficult to use, consult your dictionary for assistance. *If your dictionary does not show a*

© 1979 by Houghton Mifflin Company

spelling, do not double the final consonant. The first two are done for you.

1. occur + -ence   *occurrence*
2. travel + -er   *traveler*
3. marvel + -ous   _____
4. signal + -ing   _____
5. confer + -ing   _____
6. repel + -ent   _____
7. cancel + -able   _____
8. rebel + -ion   _____
9. forget + -able   _____
10. profit + -able   _____
11. admit + -ance   _____
12. expel + -ed   _____
13. focus + -ing   _____
14. worship + -er   _____
15. patrol + -ing   _____

THE SPELLING OF *ie* AND *ei*

A large number of spelling errors are due to confusion as to whether *ie* or *ei* should be used in a spelling. The rule is:

> *The letter* i *usually comes before* e, *except after the letter* c *or when spelling the sound of* a *heard in* neighbor *and* weigh.

If you look for the spelling of a word under *ie* and do not find it, you should always check the spelling under *ei.* For example, if you do not find *recieve* in your dictionary, you should look for *receive* and you will find the correct spelling of this word.

Exercise 4

The Spelling of ie *and* ei

The rule for spelling *ie* and *ei* may be used to find the spellings for all the following words. Use the rule and your dictionary to help you find the correct spellings of the words. The first two have been done for you.

1. n__ce   *niece*
2. rec__ve   *receive*
3. rec__pt   _____
4. fr__ght   _____
5. misch__f   _____
6. p__ce   _____
7. conc__t   _____
8. v__n   _____
9. dec__ve   _____
10. rel__f   _____
11. conc__ve   _____
12. r__ndeer   _____
13. hyg__ne   _____
14. v__l   _____
15. perc__ve   _____

ONE CONSONANT OR TWO CONSONANTS?

A fifth major spelling problem is to decide if a consonant sound is spelled by one consonant letter or by two consonant letters. This problem is illustrated by the difficulty many people have in deciding if the correct spelling is *ocassion, occasion,* or *occassion.* The confusion is due to the fact that many of our consonant sounds may be spelled by either one or two consonants. For example:

© 1979 by Houghton Mifflin Company

cabin-hobby, radish-ladder, begun-dagger, olive-silly, human-hammer, cinema-runner, open-stopper, career-carrot, resent-lesson, and hotel-bottom.

When you are not certain whether to spell a consonant sound with one consonant letter or two, you should consult your dictionary.

Exercise 5

One Consonant or Two Consonants?

Some of the following words are correctly spelled and others are incorrectly spelled. Use your dictionary, when needed, to write the correct spellings of the words on the lines provided. The first one has been done for you.

1. occassion   *occasion*
2. successful   _____
3. neccessary   _____
4. embarrassment   _____
5. dissappointment   _____
6. dissimilar   _____
7. newsstand   _____
8. essential   _____
9. dissappear   _____
10. committment   _____
11. onesself   _____
12. spaghetti   _____
13. questionnaire   _____
14. passtime   _____
15. disaggreement   _____

THE SOUND OF SCHWA

Our final major source of spelling errors is found in the fact that the sound of schwa (ə) may be spelled by *a, e, i, o,* or *u* (as well as by various vowel combinations). As you will recall from your study of the chapter on pronunciation, this is the sound you hear in such words as *alone, item, easily, lemon,* and u*pon*. *When a word contains the sound of schwa, you cannot spell the word correctly unless (1) you know how the schwa sound is spelled in the word or (2) you look for the correct spelling of the word in a dictionary.* For example, the letter that spells the sound of schwa has been left out of this word:

maint___nance

If you do not know which vowel spells the schwa sound in this word you would need to consult a dictionary if you wish to spell it correctly. The schwa sound is spelled by the letter *e: maintenance.*

Exercise 6

The Sound of Schwa

The vowels that spell the sound of schwa have been left out of the following words. Use your dictionary, when needed, to find the letter that spells the sound of schwa in these words, and write the correct spellings on the lines provided. The first one is done for you.

1. compar___son   *comparison* _____
2. cat___gory   _____
3. sens___tive   _____
4. math___matics   _____
5. calend___r   _____
6. summ___rize   _____
7. sep___rate   _____
8. def___nite   _____

(*continued*)

© 1979 by Houghton Mifflin Company

9. caf__teria   _____

10. cem__tery   _____

11. disinfect__nt _____

12. excell__nt   _____

13. sim__lar   _____

14. v__nilla   _____

15. apol__gy   _____

KEEPING A SPELLING LIST

Consider the advantages of keeping a list of the words you misspell frequently. You may use the list to refer to when you are writing, and, more importantly, you may study the words on your list to learn their spellings. There are two good ways to find words for your list:

1. Include *all* the words you misspell on papers you write in college.
2. Every time you look for the spelling of a word in your dictionary, place a check ($\sqrt{}$) in pencil next to the word. When there are three pencil checks next to a word, add the word to your spelling list and learn its spelling.

There are three ways the spellings of words may be learned: (1) by using a spelling rule, (2) by simple memorization, and (3) by using a memory-aiding trick.

If a word on your list can be learned by applying one of the four spelling rules given in this chapter, it would be best to learn the spelling by recalling the rule. For example, if you spell *sincerly* instead of *sincerely*, you should recall that a final silent *e* is usually not dropped before endings that begin with consonants.

Some spellings must be learned by simple memorization, the same way you learned to spell *Mississippi,* by saying over and over to yourself: M-i-s-s-i-s-s-i-p-p-i.

Some people like to devise memory-aiding tricks to help them remember spellings. For example, some people do not confuse *dessert* (sweet food) and *desert* (dry land) by remembering they like two desserts—*two* helps them to remember that the letter *s* appears two times in *dessert.* They then remember that if the word for "sweet food" is spelled *dessert,* then the word for "dry land" is spelled *desert.* If this appeals to you, try making up such memory-aiding tricks to help you remember the spellings of words that give you difficulty.

SOME FINAL WORDS ABOUT SPELLING

There are so many words in our language and the correct spellings of them are often so unexpected that many people become discouraged in the attempt to spell better. However, as you learned in this chapter, more accurate spelling is possible—it is within the reach of anybody who will consult a dictionary.

If you would like more suggestions to help you improve your spelling, many books have been written on the subject. Your teacher, a librarian, or a bookstore salesperson can help you find a book you can use to teach yourself the principles of good spelling. The words in your vocabulary belong to you as much as they belong to anybody else; why not learn to spell them?

© 1979 by Houghton Mifflin Company

Chapter 15   Word Origins

Most people do not give it much thought, but the words we use every day came into our language in a variety of interesting ways. Information about the origins, or *etymologies*, of words is often given in dictionaries, as the following dictionary entry suggests:

Twain (twān), **Mark.** Pen name of Samuel Langhorne **Clemens** (*see*). [From the expression *mark twain,* "by the mark two fathoms," used by Mississippi riverboat pilots in sounding shallows for minimum navigable depths.]   An etymology

The major purpose of this chapter is to develop your interest in etymologies so you will examine them when you look up words in your dictionary. Some words have such interesting origins that if you know how they came into English, it will be easy for you to learn and remember them.

In Chapters 5 through 7 you studied the etymologies of *derivatives* from base words, prefixes, and suffixes; in Chapter 9 you learned how words originated from *combining forms.* This chapter explains nine other ways words enter English.

BORROWING

Thousands of common and uncommon words are borrowed from other languages. A word is said to be borrowed when it existed in another language before it was used in English. For example, *they* was borrowed from Old Norse, *fork* was borrowed from Latin, and *beef* came from French.

Speakers of English have a long and colorful tradition of welcoming words from other languages to express new thoughts or to express existing thoughts with new words. For example, *tobacco* was borrowed from Spanish to name something that had no English name, and *perish* was borrowed from French as an additional word for our word *die*.

The history of borrowing is the history of the English-speaking people. Nearness to Europe, invasions of other peoples, trade, exploration, and colonization are some of the influences that put English speakers in contact with Norse, Dutch, German, French, Spanish, Italian, Hindi, and other languages of the world. Ever ready for a word to express a new thought or a new word to express an existing thought, English vocabulary has been greatly enriched by hundreds of years of borrowing.

The following problems will give you practice reading etymologies in dictionary listings. They will also give you some idea of the many languages that have enriched English vocabulary. Following is a sample problem, its solution, and an explanation of how it was solved:

bur·ro (bûr′ō, bŏŏr′ō) *n., pl.* **-ros.** A small donkey, especially one used as a pack animal. [Spanish, from *borrico*, donkey, from Late Latin *burricus*†, small horse.] ⎤ Borrowing

From a(n) ___*Spanish*___ word, meaning ___ ___*donkey*___ ___.

Notice that the information for the answer was taken from the beginning of the etymology. This is because the first piece of information in an etymology tells the language from which English borrowed the word. If there is additional information in an etymology, it traces the history of the word before it was borrowed by English. In the example above, *burro* was borrowed by Spanish from Late Latin.

© 1979 by Houghton Mifflin Company

Exercise 1   *Borrowing*

The directions for solving these problems are given on page 160.

1. **mas·car·a** (măs-kăr′ə) *n.* A cosmetic applied to darken the eyelashes. [Spanish *máscara,* "mask," from Italian *maschera,* possibly from Arabic *maskharah,* "buffoon." See also **mask.**]

From a(n) ———————————— word, meaning ————

——————————————————————————— .

2. **tut·ti-frut·ti** (tōō′tē-frōō′tē) *n.* **1.** A confection, especially ice cream, containing a variety of chopped candied fruits. **2.** A flavoring simulating the flavor of many fruits. —*adj.* Having a combination of fruit flavors. [Italian, "all fruits."]

From a(n) ———————————— word, meaning ————

——————————————————————————— .

3. **sa·ga** (sä′gə) *n.* **1.** An Icelandic prose narrative of the 12th and 13th centuries recounting historical and legendary events and exploits. **2.** Any long narrative. [Old Norse, a story, legend. See **sekw-³** in Appendix.*]

From a(n) ———————————— word, meaning ————

——————————————————————————— .

4. **thug** (thŭg) *n.* **1.** A cutthroat or ruffian; hoodlum; a tough. **2.** One of a former band of professional assassins in northern India. [Hindi *thag,* cheat, thief, from Sanskrit *sthaga,* robber, from *sthagati,* to cover, hide. See **steg-¹** in Appendix.*] —**thug′ger·y** *n.* —**thug′gish** *adj.*

From a(n) ———————————— word, meaning ————

——————————————————————————— .

(*continued*)

5. **waltz** (wôlts) *n.* **1.** A dance in triple time with a strong accent on the first beat. **2.** The music for this dance. —*v.* **waltzed, waltzing, waltzes.** —*intr.* **1.** To dance the waltz. **2.** To move unhesitantly and briskly; to flounce. **3.** To accomplish a task, chore, or assignment with little effort. Often used with *through: He waltzed through his exams.* —*tr.* **1.** To dance the waltz with. **2.** To lead or force to move briskly and purposefully; to march: *waltzed him into the principal's office.* [German *Walzer,* from Middle High German *walzen,* to roll, turn, dance, from Old High German *walzan,* to roll. See **wel-³** in Appendix.*] —**waltz'er** *n.*

From a(n) _____ word, meaning _____

_____ .

6. **den·tist** (děn'tĭst) *n. Abbr.* **dent.** A person whose profession is dentistry. [French *dentiste.* from *dent,* tooth. See **dentil.**]

From a(n) _____ word, meaning _____

_____ .

7. **sa·fa·ri** (sə-fä'rē) *n., pl.* **-ris.** An overland expedition, especially for hunting or exploring in East Africa. [Arabic *safarīy,* a journey, from *safara,* to travel, set out.]

From a(n) _____ word, meaning _____

_____ .

8. **stu·pen·dous** (stōō-pĕn'dəs, styōō-) *adj.* **1.** Of astounding force, volume, degree, or excellence; amazing; marvelous. **2.** Of tremendous size; huge; immense. —See Synonyms at **enormous.** [Latin *stupendus,* from *stupēre,* to be stunned. See **steu-** in Appendix.*] —**stu·pen'dous·ly** *adv.* —**stu·pen'dous·ness** *n.*

From a(n) _____ word, meaning _____

_____ .

9. **zom·bie** (zŏm'bē) *n.* Also **zom·bi** *pl.* **-bis. 1.** A snake god of voodoo cults in West Africa, Haiti, and the southern United States. **2. a.** A supernatural power or spell that according to voodoo belief can enter into and reanimate a dead body. **b.** A corpse revived in this way. **3.** One who looks or behaves like an automaton. **4.** A tall drink made of various rums, liqueur, and fruit juice. [Kongo *zumbi,* "fetish."]

From a(n) _____ word, meaning _____

_____ .

© 1979 by Houghton Mifflin Company

(continued)

10. **smor·gas·bord** (smôr′gəs-bôrd′, -bōrd′) *n.* Also *Swedish* **smör·gås·bord** (smœr′gōs-bŏŏrd′).   A meal featuring a varied number of dishes served buffet-style.   [Swedish *smörgåsbord* : *smörgås,* (open-faced) sandwich, bread and butter : *smör,* butter, from Old Norse *smör, smjör,* fat (see **smer-**³ in Appendix*) + *gås,* goose, from Old Norse *gås* (see **ghans-** in Appendix*) + *bord,* table, from Old Norse *bordh* (see **bherdh-** in Appendix*).]

From a(n) _____ word, meaning _____

_____ .

11. **ro·bot** (rō′bət, rŏb′ət) *n.*   **1.** An externally manlike mechanical device capable of performing human tasks or behaving in a human manner.   **2.** A person who works mechanically without original thought.   **3.** Any machine or device that works automatically or by remote control. Also called "automaton." [Czech, from *robota,* compulsory labor, drudgery. See **orbh-** in Appendix.*]   —**ro′bot·ism′** *n.*   —**ro′bot·is′tic** *adj.*

From a(n) _____ word, meaning _____

_____ .

12. **gar·gle** (gär′gəl) *v.* **-gled, -gling, -gles.** —*intr.*   **1.** To force exhaled air through a liquid held in the back of the mouth, with the head tilted back, in order to cleanse or medicate the mouth or throat.   **2.** To produce the sound of gargling when speaking or singing. —*tr.*   **1.** To rinse or medicate (the mouth or throat) by gargling.   **2.** To circulate or apply (a solution or medicine) by gargling.   **3.** To utter with a gargling sound. —*n.*   **1.** A medicated solution for gargling.   **2.** A gargling sound.   [Old French *gargouiller,* from *gargouille, garoule,* throat, GARGOYLE.]

From a(n) _____ word, meaning _____

_____ .

13. **car·ni·val** (kär′nə-vəl) *n.*   **1.** The season just before Lent, marked by merrymaking and feasting. See **Mardi gras.**   **2.** Any time of revelry; a festival.   **3.** A traveling amusement show, having a Ferris wheel, side shows, and the like.   [Italian *carnevale,* from Old Italian *carnelevare,* "the putting away of flesh," Shrovetide, from Medieval Latin *carnelevāmen* : Latin *carō* (stem *carn-*), flesh (see **sker-**¹ in Appendix*) + *levāre,* to raise, remove (see **legwh-** in Appendix*).]

From a(n) _____ word, meaning _____

_____ .

(continued)

14. **sham·poo** (shăm-poo′) *n., pl.* **-poos.** **1.** Any of various liquid or cream preparations of soap or detergent used to wash the hair and scalp. **2.** Any of various cleaning agents for rugs or upholstery. **3.** The act or process of washing or cleaning with shampoo. —*v.* **shampooed, -pooing, -poos.** —*tr.* To wash or clean with shampoo. —*intr.* To wash the hair with shampoo. [Hindi *chāmpo,* from *chāmpnā,* massage, press, mark, from *chāp-nā,* stamp, from *chap-nā,* to be stamped, from Indo-Aryan *chapp-* (unattested), to press, cover.]

From a(n) _____ word, meaning _____

_____ .

15. **poo·dle** (pood′l) *n.* Any of a breed of dogs originally developed in Europe as hunting dogs, having thick, curly hair, and ranging in size from the fairly large standard poodle to the very small toy poodle. [German *Pudel(hund),* "poodle (dog)," probably from Low German, perhaps "splashing dog" (because the poodle was originally trained as a water dog), akin to Old English *pudd,* ditch. See **puddle.**]

From a(n) _____ word, meaning _____

_____ .

16. **la·sa·gna** (lə-zän′yə) *pl.n.* Also **la·sa·gne.** **1.** Flat wide noodles. **2.** A dish made by baking such noodles with layers of ground meat, tomato sauce, and cheese. [Italian, from Latin *lasanum,* cooking pot, originally "chamber pot," from Greek *lasanon†.*]

From a(n) _____ word, meaning _____

_____ .

PERSON, PLACE, LITERATURE, AND MYTH

Many English words have their origin in the names of real or imaginary people or places. You probably have played with a Frisbee, but you probably do not know that the game is named for Mother Frisbie's pie plates (or, as some believe, cookie jar lids), which students at an eastern university used for playing the first game of Frisbee. And you probably say "O.K." very often but do not know that *O.K.* is believed to have come from "Old Kinderhook," a nickname for our eighth president, Martin Van Buren, who was born at Kinderhook, New York, in 1782.

© 1979 by Houghton Mifflin Company

Some of the most interesting etymologies are those of words that came from the names of real people and places and from characters in literature and mythology. The problems in Exercise 2 are based on such etymologies. Following are some sample problems that have been solved to show you how the exercises are to be done.

When an etymology is from a *person's name*, put a check (√) next to "person" and write the name of the person from whom it originated:

> **bob·by** (bŏb′ē) *n., pl.* **-bies.** *British Slang.* A policeman.   [After Sir Robert PEEL, who was Home Secretary of England when the Metropolitan Police Force was created (1828).]

person ✓   place   literature   myth

Sir Robert Peel

When an etymology is from the name of a *place*, put a check (√) next to "place" and write the name of the place from which it originated:

> **bo·lo·gna** (bə-lō′nə, -nē, -nyə) *n.* Also *informal* **ba·lo·ney** (-nē), **bo·lo·ney.** A seasoned smoked sausage made of mixed meats. [After BOLOGNA, Italy.]
> **Bo·lo·gna** (bō-lō′nyä). An industrial city and railroad center of northern Italy. Population, 482,000.

person   place ✓   literature   myth

Bologna, Italy

When an etymology is from *literature*, put a check (√) next to "literature" and write the name of the author who created the word:

> **ya·hoo** (yä′hōō, yā′-, yä-hōō′) *n., pl.* **-hoos.** A crude or brutish person. [After the *Yahoos,* a race representing humanity at large in Swift's *Gulliver's Travels.*]

person   place   literature ✓   myth

Swift

And when an etymology is from *myth*, put a check (√) next to "myth" and write the name of the mythical character or place from which it originated:

styg·i·an (stĭj′ē-ən) *adj.* Also **Styg·i·an.** **1.** Of or pertaining to the river Styx. **2. a.** Gloomy and dark. **b.** Infernal; hellish. **3.** Inviolable. [Latin *Stygius,* from Greek *Stugios,* from *Stux,* Styx. See **steu-** in Appendix.*]

Styx (stĭks) *n. Greek Mythology.* One of the rivers of Hades, across which Charon ferried the souls of the dead. [Latin, from Greek *stux.* See **steu-** in Appendix.*]

person   place   literature   myth ✓

River Styx

Exercise 2

Person, Place, Literature, and Myth

The directions for solving these problems are on pages 165–166.

1. **Je·kyll and Hyde** (jē′kəl, jĕk′əl; hīd). *Informal.* One who has quasi-schizophrenic alternating phases of pleasantness and unpleasantness. [After *The Strange Case of Dr. Jekyll and Mr. Hyde* (1886), story by R.L. Stevenson.]

person   place   literature   myth

2. **her·cu·le·an** (hûr′kyə-lē′ən, -kyo͞o′lē-ən) *adj.* **1.** Tremendously difficult or demanding: *herculean labors.* **2.** *Often capital* **H.** Resembling Hercules in size, power, or courage: *Herculean strength.* **3.** *Capital* **H.** Of or relating to Hercules.

Her·cu·les¹ (hûr′kyə-lēz′). Also **Her·a·cles** (hĕr′ə-klēz′), **Her·a·kles.** *Greek & Roman Mythology.* The son of Zeus and Alcmene, a hero of extraordinary strength who won immortality by performing the 12 labors demanded by Hera.

person   place   literature   myth

3. **bi·ki·ni** (bĭ-kē′nē) *n.* A very brief two-piece bathing suit worn by women. [French, after BIKINI atoll (referring to the "atomic" impact of the first bikinis).]

Bi·ki·ni (bĭ-kē′nē). An atoll in the Marshall Islands, in the western Pacific Ocean, the site of atomic bomb tests by the United States in 1946.

person   place   literature   myth

© 1979 by Houghton Mifflin Company

(continued)

4. **tux·e·do** (tŭk-sē′dō) *n., pl.* **-dos.** Also **Tux·e·do. 1.** A man's jacket, usually black, with satin or grosgrain lapels worn for formal or semiformal occasions. Also called "dinner jacket." **2.** A complete outfit including this jacket, black trousers with a stripe down the side, and a black bowtie.   [From the name of a country club in *Tuxedo* Park, New York, where it became popular.]

person   place   literature   myth

_____

5. **sand·wich** (sănd′wĭch, săn′-) *n.* **1.** Two or more slices of bread with meat, cheese, or other filling placed between them. **2.** An arrangement resembling an edible sandwich; for example, two slabs of one material holding a slab of different material between them, as in certain electronic devices. —*tr.v.* **sandwiched, -wiching, -wiches. 1.** To insert tightly between two things. **2.** To place in tight, alternating layers. **3.** To fit between two other things that allow little time: *sandwich a meeting between two others.* [After the Fourth Earl of *Sandwich* (1718–92), for whom sandwiches were made so that he could stay at the gambling table without interruptions for meals.]

person   place   literature   myth

_____

6. **Shan·gri·la** (shăng′grĭ-lä′) *n.* An imaginary, remote paradise on earth; utopia.   [After *Shangri-La,* the imaginary land in *Lost Horizon* (1933) by James Hilton (1900–1954).]

person   place   literature   myth

_____

7. **ser·en·dip·i·ty** (sĕr′ən-dĭp′ə-tē) *n.* The faculty of making fortunate and unexpected discoveries by accident. [Coined by Horace Walpole after the characters in the fairy tale *The Three Princes of Serendip,* who made such discoveries.] —**ser′en·dip′-i·tous** *adj.*

person   place   literature   myth

_____

(*continued*)

8. **sa·dism** (săʹdĭzʹəm, sădʹĭzʹəm) *n.* **1.** *Psychology.* The association of sexual satisfaction with the infliction of pain on others. Compare **masochism**. **2.** Broadly, delight in cruelty. [After Comte Donatien de SADE, who expounded principles of anarchic sexual violence.] —**saʹdist** *n. & adj.*
Sade (såd), Comte **Donatien Alphonse Francois de.** Known as Marquis de Sade. 1740–1814. French man of letters, novelist, and libertine.

person   place   literature   myth

_____

9. **nar·cis·sism** (närʹsə-sĭzʹəm) *n.* Also **nar·cism** (närʹsĭzʹəm). **1.** Excessive admiration of oneself. **2.** *Psychoanalysis.* An arresting of development at, or a regression to, the infantile stage of development in which one's own body is the object of erotic interest. [After NARCISSUS.] —**nar·cis·sist** (närʹsə-sĭst) *n.* —**nar·cis·sis·tic** (närʹsə-sĭsʹtĭk) *adj.*
Nar·cis·sus (när-sĭsʹəs). *Greek Mythology.* A youth who, having spurned the love of Echo, pined away in love for his own image in a pool of water and was transformed into the flower that bears his name.

person   place   literature   myth

_____

10. **jean** (jēn) *n.* **1.** A heavy, strong, twilled cotton, used in making uniforms and work clothes. **2.** *Plural.* Clothes, especially pants, made of such fabric. In this sense, also called "blue jeans." [Earlier *iene fustian, geane fustian,* from Middle English *Jene, Gene,* Genoa, where it was first made.]

person   place   literature   myth

_____

11. **tan·ta·lize** (tănʹtə-līzʹ) *tr.v.* **-lized, -lizing, -lizes.** To tease or torment by or as if by exposing to view but keeping out of reach something much desired. [From TANTALUS.] —**tanʹta·li·zaʹtion** *n.* —**tanʹta·lizʹer** *n.* —**tanʹta·lizʹing·ly** *adv.*
Tan·ta·lus (tănʹtə-ləs). *Greek Mythology.* A king who for his crimes was condemned in Hades to stand in water that receded when he tried to drink, and with fruit hanging above him that receded when he reached for it. [Latin, from Greek *Tantalos,* "bearer," "sufferer." See **tel-**¹ in Appendix.*]

person   place   literature   myth

_____

(continued)

© 1979 by Houghton Mifflin Company

12. dun·ga·ree (dŭng′gə-rē′) *n.* **1.** A sturdy, usually blue denim fabric. **2.** *Plural.* Overalls or trousers made from this fabric; blue jeans. [Hindi *dungrī,* from *Dungrī,* name of a section of Bombay where it originated.]

person   place   literature   myth

_____

13. ti·tan·ic[1] (tī-tăn′ĭk) *adj.* **1. a.** Having great stature or enormous strength; huge; colossal. **b.** Of enormous scope, power, or influence. **2.** *Capital* **T.** Of or pertaining to the Titans. [After TITAN.] —**ti·tan′i·cal·ly** *adv.*
Ti·tan[1] (tīt′n). *Greek Mythology.* One of a family of primordial gods, the children of Uranus and Gaea, overthrown and succeeded by the Olympian gods. [Middle English, the sun god, from Latin *Titan,* elder brother of Kronos and ancestor of the Titans, from Greek *Titan,* from *titō,* day, sun, from a source in Asia Minor.]

person   place   literature   myth

_____

14. mas·o·chism (măs′ə-kĭz′əm) *n.* **1.** *Psychiatry.* An abnormal condition in which sexual excitement and satisfaction depend largely on being subjected to abuse or physical pain, whether by oneself or by another. **2. a.** The deriving of pleasure from being offended, dominated, or mistreated in some way. **b.** The tendency to seek such mistreatment. **3.** The turning of any sort of destructive tendencies inward or upon oneself. Compare **sadism.** [After Leopold von Sacher-*Masoch* (1836–1895), Austrian novelist, who described it.] —**mas′o·chist** *n.* —**mas′o·chis′tic** (măs′ə-kĭs′tĭk) *adj.* —**mas′o·chis′ti·cal·ly** *adv.*

person   place   literature   myth

_____

15. boy·cott (boi′kŏt′) *tr.v.* **-cotted, -cotting, -cotts.** To abstain from using, buying, or dealing with, as a protest or means of coercion. —*n.* The act or an instance of boycotting. [After Charles C. *Boycott* (1832–1897), land agent for the Earl of Erne, County Mayo, Ireland, who was ostracized by the tenants for refusing to lower the rents.] —**boy′cott·er** *n.*

person   place   literature   myth

_____

(continued)

16. den·im (dĕn′əm) *n.* **1. a.** A coarse twilled cloth used for overalls and work uniforms. **b.** *Plural.* Garments made of coarse denim. **2.** A finer grade of material used in draperies and upholstery. [French *(serge) de Nîmes,* serge of *Nîmes,* city in southern France.]

person   place   literature   myth

_____

BLENDS, SHORTENINGS, ACRONYMS, AND IMITATIONS

Many of our words are types of shorthand. *Goodbye* is a short way of saying "God be with you," and *zing* is a short way of saying "a high-pitched sound of something moving at high speed." Problems in Exercise 3 are based on such etymologies. Following are some sample problems that have been solved to show you how they are to be done.

A *blend* is a word made from fragments of other words. When a word is a blend, put a check (√) next to "blended" and write the words from which it was created:

blotch (blŏch) *n.* **1.** A spot or blot; a splotch. **2.** A discoloration on the skin; blemish. **3.** Any of various plant diseases caused by fungi and resulting in brown or black dead areas on leaves or fruit. —*v.* **blotched, blotching, blotches.** —*tr.* To mark with blotches. Used chiefly in the past participle as an adjective: "*They were all blotched with insect bites.*" (Richard Hughes). —*intr.* To become blotched. [Probably a blend of BLOT and BOTCH.] —**blotch′i·ness** *n.* —**blotch′y** *adj.*

blended √   shortened   acronymic   imitative
_____*blot and botch*_____

This etymology states that *blotch* is probably a blend of *blot* and *botch,* but sometimes etymologies for blends do not state that they are blends. For example, an etymology for *electrocute* might read "electro- + (exe)cute," but *electrocute* would still be a blend because it is made from fragments of two words.

You use *shortened* words when you say "ad" for *advertisement* or "exam" for *examination.* When a word has been shortened, put a check (√) next to "shortened" and write the word from which it was shortened:

© 1979 by Houghton Mifflin Company

pop³ (pŏp) *adj. Informal.* **1.** Of, pertaining to, or specializing in popular music: *a pop singer.* **2.** Suggestive of **pop art** *(see).* [Short for POPULAR.]

blended   shortened ✓   acronymic   imitative

popular

An *acronym* is a word created from the initial letters of other words. When a man in the armed services is AWOL he is A(bsent) W(ith)O(ut) L(eave); AWOL is an acronym. When a word is an acronym, put a check (√) next to "acronymic" and write the words from which it was created:

GI (jē′ī′) *n., pl.* **GIs** or **GI's.** An enlisted man in or veteran of any of the U.S. armed forces. —*adj.* **1.** Pertaining to or characteristic of a GI. **2.** In conformity to or accordance with U.S. military regulations or procedures. **3.** Issued by an official U.S. military supply department. [Originally abbreviation for *galvanized iron,* army clerks' term for items such as trash cans, but later taken to be abbreviation for *general issue* or *government issue,* and extended to include all articles issued and finally soldiers themselves.]

blended   shortened   acronymic ✓   imitative

general issue or government issue

A few of our words are *imitative* of sounds; *baa, moo, bow-wow,* and *cock-a-doodle-doo,* are some of the best-known examples. When a word is imitative of a sound, put a check (√) next to "imitative" and write the sound it imitates:

thump (thŭmp) *n.* **1.** A blow with a blunt instrument. **2.** The muffled sound produced by such a blow or by a similarly muted noise; thud. —*v.* **thumped, thumping, thumps.** —*tr.* **1.** To beat with a blunt or dull instrument, or with the hand or foot, so as to produce a muffled sound or thud. **2.** To beat soundly or thoroughly; to drub. —*intr.* **1.** To hit or fall in such a way as to produce a thump; to pound. **2.** To walk with heavy steps; to stump. **3.** To throb audibly. [Imitative.] —**thump′er** *n.*

blended   shortened   acronymic   imitative ✓

a blow with a blunt instrument

Exercise 3   *Blends, Shortenings, Acronyms, and Imitations*

The directions for solving these problems are on pages 170–171.

1. **fan²** (făn) *n. Informal.* An ardent devotee or admirer, as of a sport, athletic team, or famous person. See Synonyms at **votary.** [Short for FANATIC.]

blended   shortened   acronymic   imitative

2. **Zip Code.** Also **zip code, ZIP Code.** A system designed to expedite the sorting and delivery of mail by assigning a five-digit number to each delivery area in the United States. The first three digits indicate a district, often a city, and the last two the local zone. Also called "ZIP." [Z(ONE) I(MPROVEMENT) P(ROGRAM).]

blended   shortened   acronymic   imitative

3. **Med·i·care** (mĕd′ə-kâr′) *n.* Also **med·i·care.** A program under the Social Security Administration that provides medical care for the aged. [MEDI(CAL) + CARE.]

blended   shortened   acronymic   imitative

4. **crunch** (krŭnch) *v.* **crunched, crunching, crunches.** —*tr.* 1. To chew with a noisy crackling sound. 2. To crush, grind, or tread noisily. —*intr.* 1. To chew noisily with a crackling sound. 2. To move with a crushing sound. 3. To produce or emit a crushing sound. —*n.* 1. The act or sound of crunching. 2. a. A decisive confrontation. b. A critical situation in which demand exceeds supply, creating a shortage. [Imitative.]

blended   shortened   acronymic   imitative

(continued)

© 1979 by Houghton Mifflin Company

5. mo·tel (mō-tĕl′) *n.* A hotel for motorists, usually with blocks of rooms opening directly on a parking area. Also called "motor court." [Blend of MOTOR and HOTEL.]

blended   shortened   acronymic   imitative

6. mov·ie (mōō′vē) *n. Informal.* **1.** A motion picture *(see).* **2.** A theater that shows motion pictures. **3.** *Plural.* **a.** A showing of a motion picture. Used with *the.* **b.** The motion picture indus-try. [Shortened from MOVING PICTURE.]

blended   shortened   acronymic   imitative

7. ham·burg·er (hăm′bûr′gər) *n.* Also **ham·burg** (-bûrg′). **1.** Ground or chopped meat, usually beef. **2.** A patty of such meat, cooked by frying, grilling, broiling, or baking. **3.** A sandwich made with such a patty, usually in a roll or bun. [Short for *Hamburger steak,* from HAMBURG.]

blended   shortened   acronymic   imitative

8. WAVES (wāvz). The women's reserve of the U.S. Navy. [W(OMEN) A(CCEPTED for) V(OLUNTEER) E(MERGENCY) S(ERV-ICE).]

blended   shortened   acronymic   imitative

9. scu·ba (skōō′bə) *n.* An apparatus containing compressed air and used for free-swimming underwater breathing. [S(ELF) C(ONTAINED) U(NDERWATER) B(REATHING) A(PPARATUS).]

blended   shortened   acronymic   imitative

(continued)

10. **ra·dar** (rā'där) *n.* *Electronics.* **1.** A method of detecting distant objects and determining their position, velocity, or other characteristics by analysis of very high frequency radio waves reflected from their surfaces. **2.** The equipment used in such detection. [RA(DIO) D(ETECTING) A(ND) R(ANGING).]

blended   shortened   acronymic   imitative

---

11. **smog** (smŏg, smôg) *n.* Fog that has become mixed and polluted with smoke. [Blend of SMOKE and FOG.] —**smog'gy** *adj.*

blended   shortened   acronymic   imitative

---

12. **ding-dong** (dĭng'dông', -dŏng') *n.* **1.** The peal of a bell. **2.** Any similar repeating sound. —*intr.v.* **ding-donged, -donging, -dongs.** To ring; jingle. —*adj.* Characterized by a hammering exchange, as of blows. [Imitative.]

blended   shortened   acronymic   imitative

---

13. **em·cee** (ĕm'sē') *n.* *Informal.* **A master of ceremonies** *(see).* —*v.* **emceed, -ceeing, -cees.** *Informal.* —*tr.* To serve as master of ceremonies of. —*intr.* To act as master of ceremonies. [Short for M(ASTER OF) C(EREMONIES).]

blended   shortened   acronymic   imitative

---

14. **brunch** (brŭnch) *n.* A meal eaten late in the morning as a combination of breakfast and lunch. [BR(EAKFAST) + (L)UNCH.]

blended   shortened   acronymic   imitative

(continued)

© 1979 by Houghton Mifflin Company

15. **zing** (zĭng) *n.* A brief high-pitched humming or buzzing sound, such as that made by a swiftly passing object or a taut vibrating string. —*intr.v.* **zinged, zinging, zings.** *Informal.* To make or move with such a sound. [Imitative.]

blended   shortened   acronymic   imitative

---

16. **smooch** (smōōch) *n. Slang.* A kiss. —*intr.v.* **smooched, smooching, smooches.** *Slang.* To kiss. [Perhaps imitative of a kiss.]

blended   shortened   acronymic   imitative

OTHER TYPES OF ETYMOLOGIES

Derivation, compounding, and coinage are three other ways words enter our language.

You studied *derivation* in Chapters 5 through 7. Derivation is the process by which words are created by adding prefixes or suffixes to base words. *Helpful* is a derivative created by adding the suffix *-ful* to the base word *help*.

Compounds are words made from two other words, such as *drugstore, brainwash, hitchhike,* and *lipstick.* Compounds are not given special attention in this book because you already know the basic things you should know about them.

Coinage refers to invented words. *Jello, Vaseline,* and *Frigidaire* are examples of words that were coined for the names of products. Also, many slang words were invented. *Mooch, fink, moola,* and *barf* are among the slang words that can be traced to no etymological source other than pure invention—they, too, are coinages.

The types of etymologies you studied in this book account for the origins of at least 99 percent of all the words in our language. Understanding how words enter the English vocabulary should help you not only to learn and understand the meanings of words, but also to increase your appreciation for the ways in which our thirst for new words is quenched.

Chapter 16   Synonyms

A final way to increase the number of words you use when you speak and write is to use synonyms for overworked words in everyday vocabulary. *Synonyms* are words that are similar in meaning. For example, the word *love* has many synonyms, including the following: *fondness, liking, tenderness, attachment, infatuation, adoration, admiration, yearning, affection, regard,* and *devotion.*

Before you read this chapter, evaluate the richness of the synonyms in your vocabulary by selecting a good synonym for each of the words printed in dark type in the following sentences. For example, cross out *love* in this sentence and, in the space provided, replace it with an appropriate synonym from the list given above:

———————————— Bob shows **love** for his little sister by helping her learn to read.

You might have selected *fondness, affection,* or *devotion* as a good synonym for *love* in this context. Cross out *sad, keeps, weak, strong, job,* and *reach* in the following six sentences and write good synonyms for them in the spaces provided:

———————————— 1. Five-year-old Freddie was **sad** for weeks after his dog was killed by an automobile.

———————————— 2. My employer **keeps** twenty-five dollars from my pay each month and places it in an account that draws 10 percent interest for me.

© 1979 by Houghton Mifflin Company

_____ 3. Because she was eighty years old and weighed less than one hundred pounds, Mrs. McNamara was far too **weak** to do her own housework.

_____ 4. The hikers could not have withstood the ordeal of being lost in the mountains for two weeks if they had not been as **strong** as they were.

_____ 5. A dishwashing machine makes the **job** of washing dishes more agreeable.

_____ 6. Wise people set goals for themselves that they are likely to be able to **reach**.

The words *sad, keeps, weak, strong, job,* and *reach* are all correctly used in the sentences, but there are other words that could have been used in their places. Consider the synonyms you wrote for these words to be good if they are similar to the ones in the answer key.

DEVELOPING YOUR VOCABULARY THROUGH SYNONYMS

Most English writing is made up of only a few hundred common words. Some of these words are unavoidable. It is impossible to write or speak English without using words such as *a, an, the, it, in, is, do,* and *there*. However, there are alternatives to many of the words we use over and over again. Each of the following words expresses an idea that can often be expressed better in other words: *sad, old, thin, poor, deep, sure, big, slow, fast.*

We have all known and used words such as these since we were children. They are perfectly good words, used by schoolchildren and great writers alike to express their thoughts. But if we restrict our vocabulary to words such as these, we are using a limited vocabulary and we are missing the best possible opportunity to learn and use new words.

FINDING SYNONYMS IN A DICTIONARY

One way to ensure vocabulary growth is to use a dictionary to find synonyms for overworked words in your vocabulary. For example, one student used the word *old* in this sentence:

Many people are fascinated by the **old** pyramids of Egypt.

The word *old* is used correctly in this sentence because *old* means "not new," and the pyramids are "not new." However, it occurred to the young woman who wrote this sentence that there might be a synonym for *old* that would express her idea better. When she looked up *old* in her dictionary, this is what she discovered:

old (ōld) *adj.* **older** or **elder** (ĕl′dər), **oldest** or **eldest** (ĕl′dĭst). **1.** Having lived or existed for a relatively long time; far advanced in years or life, either actually or relatively: *a feeble old man.* See Usage note at **elder. 2.** Made long ago; in existence for many years; not new: *an old book.* **3.** Of or pertaining to a long life or to persons who have had a long life: *a ripe old age.* **4.** Having or exhibiting the physical characteristics of advanced life or an aged person: *She had an old face for her years.* **5.** Having or exhibiting the wisdom of age; mature; sensible: *That child is old for her years.* **6.** Having a specified age: *She was twelve years old.* **7. a.** Belonging to a remote or former period in history; ancient: *old manuscripts.* **b.** Belonging to or being of an earlier time: *his old classmates.* **8.** Usually capital **O.** *Abbr.* **O, O.** Being the earlier or earliest of two or more related objects, stages, versions, or periods: *the Old Testament; Old High German.* **9.** *Geology.* **a.** Having become slower in flow and less vigorous in action. Said of rivers. **b.** Having become simpler in form and of lower relief. Said of land forms. **10.** Worn or dilapidated through age or use; worn-out: *an old coat.* **11.** Known through long acquaintance or use; long familiar: *an old friend.* **12.** Dear or cherished through long acquaintance. Used as a term of affection or cordiality: *good old Harry.* **13.** Skilled or able through long experience; practiced: *He was an old hand at shipbuilding.* **14.** *Informal.* Fine; excellent; great: *We had a high old time.* —*n.* **1.** Former times; yore: *in days of old.* **2.** An individual of a specified age. Used in combination: *a five-year-old.* [Middle English *old, ald,* Old English *eald, ald.* See **al-³** in Appendix.*] —**old′ness** *n.*

→ *Definitions*

Synonyms: *old, elderly, aged, venerable, superannuated.* These terms are compared in their application to persons. *Old,* though ostensibly general, often stresses advanced years strongly. *Elderly* specifies the period past late middle age without necessarily implying marked decline. *Aged* emphasizes advanced years, and often suggests infirmity. *Venerable* suggests dignity and qualities, associated with age, that are worthy of great respect. *Superannuated,* in contrast, applies narrowly to the state of being pensioned or retired, or, more generally, to one figuratively discarded or outmoded.

→ *Synonyms for people*

Olden, ancient, archaic, obsolete, obsolescent, antique, antiquated, and *old-fashioned* are terms that are applied principally to inanimate objects and historical associations. *Old* is the general term. *Olden* connotes a bygone age, often with some nostalgia. *Ancient* pertains to the distant past, and usually to what no longer exists. *Archaic* similarly specifies a very early, often primitive, period, but does not always imply the fact of being discarded; archaic language, though not in general use, is preserved for historical value and limited application. *Obsolete* indicates merely the fact of having passed from use, and *obsolescent* the state of becoming obsolete. *Antique* may indicate association with the ancient past; more often it characterizes that which is valued for its membership in a class of things from the more recent past. *Antiquated,* in contrast, indicates that which is discarded as now out-of-date or discredited. *Old-fashioned* pertains more generally to something from the recent past that is no longer in vogue or general use; it does not invariably imply low regard or the fact of having been discarded.

→ *Synonyms for objects*

© 1979 by Houghton Mifflin Company

After studying this entry for *old,* the student decided *ancient* would probably be better than *old* in her sentence. She looked up the meaning of *ancient* and was assured it is an excellent adjective for describing many things belonging to a time more than 1,500 years ago. She rewrote her sentence:

> Many people are fascinated by the **ancient** pyramids of Egypt.

This is the strategy for expanding your vocabulary by using a dictionary:

> *When you use a word that you have used all your life, ask yourself if there might not be a synonym to express your thought. Look up the word you are questioning in a dictionary to determine if there are synonyms which can be used in its place.*

Sometimes there will not be a discussion of synonyms immediately following the word you investigate. If you wanted a synonym for *smart,* you might find a cross-reference that tells you to look up the word *intelligent:*

smart (smärt) *intr.v.* **smarted, smarting, smarts. 1.** To cause a sharp, usually superficial, stinging pain, as an acrid liquid or a slap. **2.** To be the source of such a pain, as a wound. **3.** To feel such a pain. **4.** To suffer acutely, as from mental distress, wounded feelings, remorse, or the like: *"No creature smarts so little as a fool."* (Pope). **5.** To suffer or pay a heavy penalty. Usually used with *for.* —*n.* Sharp mental or physical pain. —*adj.* **smarter, smartest. 1. a.** Characterized by sharp, quick thought; bright. **b.** Amusingly or impertinently clever; witty: *a smart answer.* **2.** Characterized by sharp, quick movement; energetic: *a smart pace.* **3.** Characterized by sharpness in dealings; shrewd: *a smart businessman.* **4.** Characterized by sharpness in dress; trim; elegant. **5.** Associated with, characteristic of, or patronized by persons of fashion; fashionable: *a smart restaurant.* —See Synonyms at **intelligent.** [Middle English *smarten, smerten,* Old English *smeortan.* See smerd- in Appendix.*] —**smart′ly** *adv.* —**smart′ness** *n.*

Cross-reference to discussion of synonyms

Sometimes there is no cross-reference to a discussion of synonyms. If you wanted to find synonyms for *thin,* to describe a person, you would need to use the synonyms given in the appropriate definition:

thin (thĭn) *adj.* **thinner, thinnest. 1.** Having a relatively small distance between opposite sides or surfaces. **2.** Not great in diameter or cross section; fine: *a thin strand of hair.* **3.** Lean or slender of figure. **4.** Not dense or concentrated; sparse. **5.** Not rich or heavy in consistency: *thin gravy.* **6.** Sparsely supplied or provided; scanty: *a thin menu.* **7.** Lacking force or substance; flimsy: *a thin attempt.* **8.** Lacking resonance or fullness; tinny. Said of sound or tone. **9.** Lacking radiance or intensity. Said of light or color. **10.** *Photography.* Not having enough contrast to make satisfactory prints. Said of a negative. —*adv.* So as to be thin; thinly. —*v.* **thinned, thinning, thins.** —*intr.* To become thin or thinner. —*tr.* To make thin or thinner. [Middle English *thinne,* Old English *thynne.* See **ten-** in Appendix.*] —**thin′ness** *n.*

Look up *lean* or *slender* to see if synonyms are discussed.

If you looked up *lean* in this dictionary, you would find a discussion of *lean, spare, skinny, scrawny, lank, lanky, raw-boned,* and *gaunt.*

Finally, you can also find synonyms in a thesaurus. Figure 16.1 shows the entry for *hate* from *The New American Roget's College Thesaurus,* which is published in paperback. Notice that the thesaurus gives synonyms but does not tell the meanings of words. If you wanted a synonym for *hate* but did not know the exact meanings of *abhorrence, loathing, alienation, estrangement,* or *enmity,* you would need to consult a dictionary for the meanings of these words. It is for this reason that for most people a good desk dictionary is the best source of information about synonyms.

FIGURE 16.1 The Entry for the Word *Hate* **from** *The New American Roget's College Thesaurus.* **A thesaurus gives synonyms for words but does not give the meanings of synonyms. (From THE NEW AMERICAN ROGET'S COLLEGE THESAURUS in dictionary form by Albert H. Morehead. Copyright © 1958, 1962 by Albert H. Morehead. Reprinted by arrangement with The New American Library, Inc., New York, N.Y.)**

HATE

Nouns—**1,** hate, hatred, abhorrence, loathing; disaffection, disfavor; alienation, estrangement, coolness; enmity, hostility, animosity, RESENTMENT; umbrage, pique, irritation, grudge; dudgeon, spleen, spite, despite, venom, venomousness, bitterness, bad blood; acrimony; malice, MALEVOLENCE, implacability, REVENGE; repugnance, DISLIKE, odium, unpopularity; detestation, antipathy.
2, object of hatred, abomination, aversion, *bête noire;* enemy.
Verbs—**1,** hate, detest, despise, abominate, abhor, loathe; shrink from, view with horror, hold in abomination, revolt against, execrate; DISLIKE.
2, excite *or* provoke hatred, be hateful; repel, envenom, incense, irritate, rile; horrify.
Adjectives—**1,** averse, set against, hostile; bitter, acrimonious (see DISCOURTESY); implacable, revengeful (see RETALIATION); invidious, spiteful, malicious (see MALEVOLENCE).
2, hated, despised, unloved, unbeloved, unlamented, unmourned, disliked; forsaken, rejected, lovelorn, jilted.
3, obnoxious, hateful, abhorrent, despicable, odious, abominable, repulsive, loathsome, offensive, shocking; disgusting, disagreeable.
4, be unfriendly, on bad terms, estranged, *etc.*
Antonym, see LOVE.

© 1979 by Houghton Mifflin Company

PRACTICE PROBLEMS

The practice problems for this chapter should help you better understand how you can use the discussions of synonyms in dictionaries to expand your vocabulary. They consist of a dictionary discussion of synonyms for a common word, followed by three sentences for which synonyms need to be supplied. Follow these directions for doing the problems:

1. Do not use the word in capital letters as the answer to a problem.

2. Do not use a synonym more than once for a set of problems.

Here is a sample problem, its solution, and a discussion of how it was solved:

> POOR
>
> **Synonyms:** *poor, indigent, impoverished, destitute.* These describe a person without income. *Poor* is the most general and means, broadly, lacking money or means for an adequate existence. One who is *poor* is usually characteristically or continually so. *Indigent* more specifically refers to one in straitened circumstances but not in total adversity. Like *poor*, it sometimes denotes a social class. *Impoverished* means abjectly poor, usually conspicuously so. The strongest of these words is *destitute*, which suggests poverty due to misfortune and particularly implies urgent need.

1. You would cringe to see the shacklike houses and shabby clothing of the *impoverished* people in some parts of this country.

2. They escaped from the fire with nothing but the clothes they were wearing; they had lost everything they owned and were left *destitute* .

3. There is growing concern for the *indigent* migrant workers in this country who must work long hours under difficult circumstances to earn barely enough to survive.

Notice that the word in capital letters (POOR) was not used as an answer to a problem and that no synonym was used more than one time.

© 1979 by Houghton Mifflin Company

Exercise 1   *Synonyms*

The directions for solving these problems are given under "Practice Problems."

FAT

Synonyms: *fat, obese, corpulent, fleshy, stout, portly, pudgy, rotund, plump, chubby.* These adjectives mean having an abundance of flesh, often to excess. *Fat* always implies excessive weight and is generally unfavorable in its connotations. *Obese* is employed principally in medical usage with reference to extreme overweight, and *corpulent* is a more general term for the same condition. *Fleshy* implies an abundance of flesh that is not necessarily disfiguring. *Stout* and *portly* are sometimes used as polite terms to describe fatness. *Stout,* in stricter application, suggests a thickset, bulky person, and *portly,* one whose bulk is combined with an imposing bearing. *Pudgy* describes one who is thickset and dumpy. *Rotund* suggests roundness of figure in a squat person. *Plump* is applicable to a pleasing fullness of figure, especially in women. *Chubby* implies abundance of flesh, usually not to excess.

1. Whenever somebody implies that his wife is fat, Henry always says, "I like _____ women."

2. The doctor told her patient that he was _____ and should go on a diet immediately.

3. At one time it was considered distinguished for a gentleman of middle years to be _____ .

QUIET

Synonyms: *still, quiet, silent, noiseless, hushed, tranquil.* These adjectives refer to the relative absence of sound or movement. *Still* can apply to what is without sound or activity or both, as can *quiet. Still* is usually the more emphatic in all senses; *quiet* often implies merely the absence of noise, bustle, or customary activity. *Silent* refers only to what is without sound or noise. Like *noiseless* and *hushed,* it makes no clear indication with respect to movement or the absence thereof. *Noiseless* can mean without sound but usually implies freedom from excessive or disturbing sound. *Hushed* suggests a sudden condition of silence, especially one following noise or excitement. *Tranquil* primarily implies calm and lack of agitated movement.

4. The noisy crowd became _____ when it realized the man was serious in his attempt to jump from the bridge.

5. We spread our blanket in a _____ field, beneath a shady tree.

6. I knew that if I moved he would kill me, so I was absolutely

_____ .

(continued)

Synonyms: high, tall, lofty, towering, elevated. These adjectives mean standing out or otherwise distinguished because of height. *High* and *tall,* the most general terms, are sometimes interchangeable. In general *high* refers to what rises a considerable distance from a base or is situated at a level well above another level considered as a base: *a high mountain; a high ceiling; a high shelf. Tall* describes what rises to a considerable

HIGH   extent; it often refers to living things and to what has great height in relation to breadth or in comparison with like things: *a tall man; tall trees; a tall building. Lofty* describes what is imposingly or inspiringly high. *Towering* suggests height that causes awe or makes something stand out conspicuously. *Elevated* stresses height in relation to immediate surroundings; it refers principally to being raised or situated above a normal level or above the average level of an area.

7. The mayor and several other officials were seated on a(n)

_____ platform so they could be seen by the crowd.

8. The fields, lakes, and towns below were miniaturized in our

view from the _____ peak of Mt. Rainier.

9. I was astonished when I visited lower Manhattan and saw the

buildings of the World Trade Center _____

above me.

Synonyms: small, little, diminutive, minute, miniature, minuscule, tiny, wee, petite. These adjectives describe persons or things whose physical size is markedly below that of the average. *Small* and *little* can often be used interchangeably. In general, *small* has the wider application; with reference to physical size, *little* is usually more emphatic in implying sharp reduction from the average. *Little* is sometimes used also to add a sense of

SMALL   charm, endearment, or pathos to the term modified. *Diminutive* means very, often abnormally, small. *Minute* describes what is small to the point of being difficult to see. *Miniature* applies to a representation of something on a greatly reduced scale. *Minuscule* refers to what is very small, and is occasionally used in the sense of miniature. *Tiny* and *wee* both mean exceptionally small and are often interchangeable, though *wee* generally implies endearment or humor. *Petite* is applied principally to the feminine figure in the sense of small and trim.

10. At age forty-five General Tom Thumb was no taller than a

four-year-old; his fame was due to his _____ size.

11. We were amazed to hear a deep, booming voice come from

such a _____ woman.

12. Medical technology has developed equipment that enlarges

_____ nerves so they can be seen and sewn

back together if they become severed.

© 1979 by Houghton Mifflin Company

Exercise 2   _Synonyms_

The directions for solving these problems are given just before the first exercise for this chapter.

> **Synonyms:** _slow, dumb, stupid, dull, obtuse, dense, crass._ These adjectives mean lacking in mental acuity. _Slow_ and the informal _dumb_ imply chronic sluggishness of perception or understanding; _stupid_ and _dull_ occasionally suggest a mere temporary state. DUMB _Stupid_ and _dumb_ also can refer to individual actions that are extremely foolish. _Obtuse_ implies insensitivity or unreceptiveness to instruction. _Dense_ suggests a mind that is virtually impenetrable or incapable of grasping even elementary ideas. _Crass_ refers especially to stupidity marked by coarseness or tastelessness.

1. The boss told them they would receive twenty-five-dollar raises if they could manage to arrive at work on time, but they are so

_____ they continue to come in ten minutes late.

2. I thought it was _____ of Jim to keep insisting Marjorie have a glass of champagne—he knows she never drinks.

3. It was _____ of them to try to reconcile their daughter and son-in-law; the marriage was over, and there was no way it could be saved.

> **Synonyms:** _sure, certain, confident, assured._ These adjectives are compared as they apply to persons who do not doubt their own abilities. _Sure_ and _certain_ are frequently used interchangeably. _Sure_, however, is the more subjective term, whereas SURE _certain_ may imply belief based on experience or established evidence. _Confident_ suggests belief founded on faith or reliance in oneself or in others. _Assured_ suggests confidence or certainty based on knowledge that doubt has been removed.

4. After eating in every restaurant within miles of school, I am

_____ The Shed has the best food.

5. Nobody is perfect, but I am _____ most presidents of this country have tried to govern to the best of their ability.

6. John thought he had broken his hand; but after the doctor examined him, he was _____ there was no fracture.

(_continued_)

Synonyms: *strange, peculiar, odd, queer, quaint, outlandish, singular, eccentric.* These adjectives describe persons or things that are notably unusual. *Strange* refers especially to what is unfamiliar, unknown, or inexplicable. *Peculiar,* though often applied to anything unusual, is most applicable to what distinguishes a given person or thing from others. *Odd* suggests the quality of not fitting in, or lack of accord with associates, surroundings, or circumstances. *Queer* implies difference from the norm. *Quaint* often refers to peculiarity that seems old-fashioned but endearing. *Outlandish* suggests alien appearance or manner and often implies uncouthness. *Singular* describes what is unique, unparalleled, or unusual and thus arouses curiosity or wonder. *Eccentric* refers particularly to striking peculiarity of behavior.

STRANGE

7. One could not help noticing the _____

growth of hair from her chin and wondering why she did not have

it removed.

8. The Amish have a(n) _____ custom of

traveling by horse and buggy rather than by automobile.

9. Egbert always ran around campus in a straw hat, bright

green cape, and red knickers with no apparent concern that his

_____ costume made him the joke of the

school.

Synonyms: *hard, difficult, arduous, intricate, troublesome.* These adjectives are closely related when they mean requiring great physical or mental effort. *Hard* and *difficult,* the most general terms, are interchangeable in many examples, but *difficult* is often the more appropriate where a challenge requiring special skills or ingenuity is involved. *Arduous* refers to what involves burdensome labor or persistent effort, especially physical. *Intricate* describes what is difficult because its complexity makes great mental demands. *Troublesome* implies demands that cause vexation, worry, or anxiety.

HARD

10. It is remarkable that this country had such a large number of

pioneers who were willing to accept the _____

life of the wilderness.

11. I marvel that even an army of workers could solve the

_____ problems involved in compiling a

dictionary.

12. It is _____ for many people to develop the

habit of saving part of what they earn.

© 1979 by Houghton Mifflin Company

Exercise 3

Synonyms

The directions for solving these problems are given just before the first exercise for this chapter.

HAPPY

Synonyms: *glad, happy, cheerful, lighthearted, joyful, joyous.* These adjectives mean in good spirits. *Glad* often has reference to the strong feeling that results from gratification of a wish or from satisfaction with immediate circumstances. *Happy*, a more general term, can describe almost any condition of good spirits, temporary or sustained. *Cheerful* suggests good spirits made obvious by an outgoing nature, and *lighthearted* makes more explicit the absence of care. *Joyful* and *joyous*, the strongest of these terms, suggest extremely high spirits or a strong sense of fulfillment or satisfaction.

1. I was _____ that the professor did not call on me today, because I was not prepared.

2. Judy is always so _____ that it lifts her friends' spirits just to see her.

3. Reeva and Tom spent years trying to adopt a child, so the baby's first day in their home was an especially _____ one.

SHOW

Synonyms: *show, display, expose, parade, exhibit, flaunt.* These verbs mean to present something to view. *Show* is the most general, since it makes no clear implication as to manner or method of presentation. *Display* usually suggests an attempt to present something to best advantage, but it can imply ostentation or even the making obvious of something better concealed, such as ignorance. *Expose* usually involves uncovering or bringing from concealment or unmasking. *Parade* generally suggests a blatant or boastful presentation. *Exhibit* implies open, rather formal presentation that invites inspection. *Flaunt* implies a prideful, arrogant attempt to gain attention.

4. He claims he is telling the truth, but the facts _____ this man to be a liar.

5. Shops now _____ Christmas cards and wrappings early in November.

6. We greatly admired Richard's intelligence until he began to _____ his brilliance by making fools of those with less ability.

(*continued*)

Synonyms: *teach, instruct, educate, tutor, train, school, discipline, drill.* These verbs mean to impart knowledge or skill. *Teach* is the most widely applicable, since it can refer to any such act of communicating. *Instruct* usually suggests methodical direction in a specific subject or area. *Educate* is comprehensive and implies a wide area of learning, achieved either by experience or, more often, by formal instruction in many subjects. *Tutor* usually refers to private instruction of one student or a small group. *Train* generally implies concentration on particular skills intended to fit a person, or sometimes an animal, for a desired role. *School* and *discipline* now usually refer to training in modes of behavior. *School* often implies indoctrination, not necessarily in an unfavorable sense, and an arduous learning process. *Discipline* usually refers to teaching of control, especially self-control. *Drill* implies rigorous instruction or training, often by repetition of a routine.

TEACH

7. Bob's parents take him to a different part of the United States each year in order to _____ him about life and places in his country.

8. Over the years, the army has developed efficient methods to _____ men to become combat soldiers.

9. All through school there are teachers who_____ students in writing improvement.

Synonyms: *tired, weary, exhausted, fatigued, jaded, bushed.* These adjectives apply to conditions in which physical strength or strength of spirit is depleted, usually as the result of exertion or tribulation. *Tired* is the general, nonspecific term. *Weary,* like *tired,* is applicable to deficiency of strength or spirit, but often carries a stronger implication of discontent resulting from what is burdensome, irksome, boring, or the like. *Exhausted* and *fatigued* are much stronger terms. *Exhausted* specifies complete or nearly complete expenditure of physical strength. *Fatigued* implies great, though not necessarily complete, expenditure of physical or mental power. *Jaded* refers largely to dullness of spirit, often resulting from overindulgence. *Bushed* informally suggests temporary deficiency of strength resulting usually from physical exertion.

TIRED

10. Most of the runners who started the twenty-six-mile race became too _____ to finish it.

11. By the end of August, Fred was _____ of working in the factory and eager for school to begin.

12. After six hours at her desk, Daisy was_____ from studying so she went out to visit with friends.

© 1979 by Houghton Mifflin Company

ANSWER KEY

This is a partial answer key for you to use to assure yourself that you are solving problems correctly. If the answers you write are very different from the ones in this key, you are answering questions incorrectly. In such a case, reread the information that explains how to solve the problems.

CHAPTER 2
FINDING WORD MEANINGS
IN SENTENCES

EXERCISE 1 (P. 17)

1. taxonomy: classification system
2. objective: reporting what is factual or real

EXERCISE 2 (P. 19)

1. edifice: building (not structure or skyscraper—not all structures are buildings, and skyscrapers are not the only edifices)
2. surreptitiously: secretly, slyly, covertly

EXERCISE 3 (P. 21)

1. enervated: weakened, exhausted
2. acquitted: found not guilty, cleared, freed

EXERCISE 4 (P. 23)

1. extricate: release, free, disengage
2. incensed: angered, enraged

CHAPTER 3
FINDING WORD MEANINGS
IN TEXTBOOKS

EXERCISE 1 (PP. 27–28)

1. *skim-the-cream pricing:* A product is first sold at the highest price at which it can be sold, and the price is later reduced when the product can no longer be sold at the highest price.

EXERCISE 2 (PP. 35–36)

Your answers will have the appearance of the answers for the first exercise in this chapter, but they will be different from the responses of all other students.

CHAPTER 4
FINDING WORD MEANINGS
IN PICTURES

PRETEST; CONTEXT AND PICTURES (PP. 39; 40–43)

1. a
2. b
3. d
4. a
5. d

CHAPTER 5
PREFIXES

EXERCISE 1 (PP. 51–52)

1. remove the knot from
2. judges who cannot be corrupted
6. get off, come down from
8. People who are not members
11. care after the operation

EXERCISE 2 (PP. 53–54)

1. trips across oceans
2. bad nutrition

EXERCISE 3 (PP. 55–56)

1. organizations that do not make a profit
2. interpreted too many questions incorrectly (or badly, wrongly)

EXERCISE 4 (PP. 57–58)

1. walk after breakfast
2. insist again, insist once more

© 1979 by Houghton Mifflin Company

CHAPTER 6
BASE WORDS

EXERCISE 1 (P. 63)

1. distribute   no change
2. frustrate   *e* dropped
3. ally   *y* to *i*
5. angle   other change

EXERCISE 2 (P. 65)

1. decent   other change
2. measure   *e* dropped

EXERCISE 3 (P. 67)

1. rely   *y* to *i*
4. distribute *e* dropped

CHAPTER 7
SUFFIXES

EXERCISE 1 (PP. 73–74)

1. digest, digestive
2. distractible, distract

EXERCISE 2 (PP. 75–76)

1. predict, predictable
2. experimentation, Experimental

EXERCISE 3 (PP. 77–78)

1. observe, observant
2. mystify, mysterious

CHAPTER 8
FINDING WORD MEANINGS
FROM WORD STRUCTURE
AND CONTEXT

EXERCISE 1 (PP. 81–82)

1. context—using words to impress rather than to express their thoughts clearly
5. context—clouding; word structure—*obscure* is base word
7. word structure—against personnel or people

EXERCISE 2 (PP. 83–84)

1. word structure—*grammar* is base word; context—sentence indicates they are people. Grammarians must be people who specialize in grammar.
2. word structure—not allowed, forbidden

EXERCISE 3 (PP. 85–86)

1. word structure—exceedingly sensitive
2. context—guilty

CHAPTER 9
COMBINING FORMS

EXERCISE 1 (PP. 89–91)

1. b
2. b

EXERCISE 2 (PP. 93–94)

2. archaeology, archaeologist
3. audiology, audiologist

EXERCISE 3 (PP. 95–96)

2. thunder, lightning, storms (not stars)
10. being alone (not the number *one*)

EXERCISE 4 (PP. 97–98)

2. benign
10. mother

EXERCISE 5 (P. 99)

Answers will vary.

CHAPTER 10
DICTIONARIES

EXERCISE 1 (PP. 109–110)

1. 1
2. 2
3. 3

EXERCISE 2 (PP. 111–112)

1. 7
2. 6
3. 1

EXERCISE 3 (PP. 113–114)

1. 5
2. 1
3. 6

EXERCISE 4 (PP. 115–116)

1. 1
2. 3
3. 2

CHAPTER 11
OTHER REFERENCE SOURCES

Your answers to the exercise on pages 125–126 will be different from the answers of all others who do this activity. If you have difficulty, be certain to ask a librarian for assistance.

CHAPTER 12
LEARNING NEW WORDS

The solutions to the three exercises on pages 134 and 137 will vary. Evaluate your cards or notes on (1) the extent to which they correspond to the examples given in Chapter 12 and (2) their usefulness to you in learning the meanings of words. If your cards or notes were not useful to you for learning words, you probably either did not make good ones or failed to study them in the way suggested in Chapter 12.

Notice in Exercise 3 (p. 137) that you should include *pronuncia-*

© 1979 by Houghton Mifflin Company

PROPERTY OF
COMMUNICATION SKILLS CENTER
OHIO NORTHERN UNIVERSITY

tions only when you do not know them, *etymologies* only when they are helpful to learning the meaning of a word, and *synonyms* only when words have synonyms.

**CHAPTER 13
PRONUNCIATION**

EXERCISE 1 (PP. 140–141)

3. said
4. hop
5. plane (or plain)

EXERCISE 2 (P. 142)

4. foot
5. fool
9. fume

EXERCISE 3 (P. 144)

4. ease
5. fight
6. ghost

EXERCISE 4 (PP. 145–146)

2. action
3. addition

EXERCISE 5 (PP. 146–147)

2. character
3. Chicago

**CHAPTER 14
SPELLING**

EXERCISE 1 (P. 150)

If dictionaries give two spellings for a word, the first spelling given in most dictionaries is the one used here. All the spellings follow the rule except for these four words:

5. judgment
8. acreage

11. argument
15. acknowledgment

EXERCISE 2 (PP. 151–152)

All the spellings follow the rule except for these three words:

6. slyness
9. studying

14. shyly

EXERCISE 3 (P. 153)

If dictionaries give two spellings for a word, the first spelling given in most dictionaries is the one used here.

3. marvelous

5. conferring

EXERCISE 4 (P. 154)

3. receipt
4. freight

EXERCISE 5 (P. 155)

2. successful
3. necessary

EXERCISE 6 (PP. 156-157)

2. category
3. sensitive

**CHAPTER 15
WORD ORIGINS**

EXERCISE 1 (PP. 161-164)

1. Spanish; mask
2. Italian; all fruits

EXERCISE 2 (PP. 166-170)

1. literature; R. L. Stevenson
2. myth; Hercules
3. place; Bikini, an atoll in the Pacific Ocean
5. person; Fourth Earl of Sandwich

EXERCISE 3 (PP. 172-175)

1. shortened; fanatic
2. acronymic; *zone improvement program*
3. blended; *medi*cal + *care*
4. imitative; a noisy crackling sound

**CHAPTER 16
SYNONYMS**

PRETEST (PP. 176-177)

1. depressed, desolate, or miserable
2. withholds, reserves, or retains
3. feeble, frail, or decrepit
4. tough, sturdy, or hale
5. ´chore or task
6. attain or achieve

EXERCISE 1 (PP. 183-184)

1. plump
2. obese, corpulent
3. portly, (stout). The parentheses indicate a possible but less desirable answer.

EXERCISE 2 (PP. 185-186)

1. dense, (slow). The parentheses indicate a possible but less desirable answer.
2. crass, obtuse
3. stupid, obtuse

EXERCISE 3 (PP. 187-188)

1. glad
2. cheerful, lighthearted
3. joyous, joyful

ABCDEFGHIJ—M—798

© 1979 by Houghton Mifflin Company